Getting Started with Clickteam Fusion

Create compelling 2D games using Clickteam Fusion

Jürgen Brunner

PUBLISHING

BIRMINGHAM - MUMBAI

Getting Started with Clickteam Fusion

First published: March 2014

Production Reference: 1130314

Published by Packt Publishing Ltd.
Livery Place
35 Livery Street
Birmingham B3 2PB, UK.

ISBN 978-1-78328-361-3

www.packtpub.com

Cover Image by John Michael Harkness (jtothem@gmail.com)

Credits

Author
Jürgen Brunner

Reviewers
Jenna Brown

Albert Chen

Timothy Hess

Acquisition Editor
Llewellyn Rozario

Content Development Editor
Anila Vincent

Technical Editors
Tanvi Bhatt

Shiny Poojary

Copy Editors
Sarang Chari

Brandt D'Mello

Project Coordinator
Mary Alex

Proofreader
Ameesha Green

Indexer
Rekha Nair

Production Coordinator
Conidon Miranda

Cover Work
Conidon Miranda

About the Author

Jürgen Brunner is currently working as a game designer and an indie developer in Austria and Germany. You can definitely call him a *video game enthusiast*, which he has been since the 1980s. Remembering the first gaming sessions on a friend's *Amiga 500*, he tries to stay as connected as possible to the main goal of every game: fun!

He studied game design and music at the University of Applied Sciences in Salzburg, and received his degree in 2010 with the diploma thesis "Jump 'n' Run Evolution".

While working as a researcher at the **Pervasive experience lab (P.e.l.s)** in his former university, he had the privilege of exploring augmented reality and pervasive games as well as Kinect hacks.

Jürgen made his way to the professional gaming industry as a game and level designer in 2012. Besides this, he also works on his own indie games. His love and passion for retro graphics, music, and art can be experienced in every new game and in every new song. The greatest success of his indie career so far might be the release of the award winning game *Pitiri 1977* on Steam in 2014.

Besides working on games, he is also a passionate musician. As well as playing six instruments, Jürgen still tries to spend every free minute on music and sound design, or with his band SaberRider.

Thanks to Ela, Chrisi, Marti, and Lina. Because of you guys, I feel like Stephen King while writing a book about video games!

About the Reviewers

Jenna Brown is a graduate from Emily Carr University of Art and Design with a Bachelor of Fine Arts in Animation. When she was young, she learned coding online, and since then has worked to create her own games and projects. She has taught the subject of game designing at several schools, including Digital Media Academy, and taught animation at Capilano University at Summer Fun Camps and Reel to Real Film Festival.

> I would like to acknowledge my grandfather RK Brown for encouraging me to learn and teaching me that learning new things is a wonderful lifelong adventure. I would also like to acknowledge my family, friends, teachers, students, my mother Shannon, and Toan for encouraging me to create, learn, and teach. Without these people, I would not be creating games, nor would I be reviewing this book. They have my deepest thanks.

Albert Chen is an Assistant Professor in the Game Design and Development program at Cogswell College in Sunnyvale, California. He has led students in developing serious games using game engines for the Boeing Company, Neurosky, and Ericsson. His team won the Boeing Performance Excellence Award in 2008.

Prior to joining Cogswell in 2007, Mr. Chen was a professional game developer for over twelve years working at Electronic Arts, LucasArts, Factor 5, and the 3DO Company. He has a BA in International Relations from UC Davis and will receive a Master of Arts in Entrepreneurship and Innovation from Cogswell College in 2014.

> I would like to thank my family for their love and support: Joy, Kayli, Brandon, and my mother, Sin-Hing Chen.

Timothy Hess has been creating video games since he was a teenager. He began making simple games using Game Factory, and later using Clickteam Fusion. This love of video games and their creation led him to the University of Baltimore, where he earned a BS in Simulation and Digital Entertainment. Recently, he received a MA in Interactive Design and Game Development from the Savannah College of Art and Design. Currently, he is working on a space exploration game using Clickteam Fusion and numerous other endeavors with teams of his colleagues online. Some of his work can be seen by visiting TimHess3D.com.

www.PacktPub.com

Support files, eBooks, discount offers and more

You might want to visit www.PacktPub.com for support files and downloads related to your book.

Did you know that Packt offers eBook versions of every book published, with PDF and ePub files available? You can upgrade to the eBook version at www.PacktPub.com and as a print book customer, you are entitled to a discount on the eBook copy. Get in touch with us at service@packtpub.com for more details.

At www.PacktPub.com, you can also read a collection of free technical articles, sign up for a range of free newsletters and receive exclusive discounts and offers on Packt books and eBooks.

http://PacktLib.PacktPub.com

Do you need instant solutions to your IT questions? PacktLib is Packt's online digital book library. Here, you can access, read and search across Packt's entire library of books.

Why Subscribe?

- Fully searchable across every book published by Packt
- Copy and paste, print and bookmark content
- On demand and accessible via web browser

Free Access for Packt account holders

If you have an account with Packt at www.PacktPub.com, you can use this to access PacktLib today and view nine entirely free books. Simply use your login credentials for immediate access.

Table of Contents

Preface

When I was a kid I wanted to know how to create my own video games. Unfortunately, I wasn't much of a programmer and nobody could really tell me where or how to start my development career. The gaming scene has mainly been appreciated by slightly nerdy kids like myself and the gaming industry has been much smaller than today.

Well, what can I say, times have changed! And video games are a well-respected art form, business, and even lifestyle these days. Together with this scene, the ways of game development have changed and it is much easier to learn how to create video games today.

Of course, not everyone can be a great programmer. You might have great game ideas and artistic skills, but programming, well, let's say it's not your flagship. This is exactly the moment where this very book and Fusion enters your life! Learn how to create awesome 2D games without knowing a scripting language. Understand the basics of game development with Fusion and acquire a solid basis in designing games. Follow your passion and start to create the games you've always wanted to play!

What this book covers

Chapter 1, *The Basics of Fusion*, will introduce you to the world of game development with Fusion by Clickteam. Learning a new tool is a challenging task. You'll learn the basics of the tool's user interface and how to begin developing games.

Chapter 2, *The Editors of Fusion – Your First Game!*, will give you an overview of the different editors and their usage. Everything in Fusion is constructed to be very intuitive and easy to learn. Still it takes some time to understand the mechanics of the tool.

Chapter 3, Movements, Animations, and Graphics, is all about movement and how to breathe life into your game. Understand the basics of animations and the animation editor. One of the most essential benefits of Fusion are its built-in movement templates, which you are about to learn.

Chapter 4, Using Extensions and Animations, will teach you how to use colliders and trigger animations. The backbone of Fusion is its extension and objects system. Learn how important it is to use the advanced platform movement object.

Chapter 5, Creating Enemy Behavior and Health Bars in the Right Resolution, will help you to decide on a resolution and the right interface for your game. Game development is not all about turning cool ideas into games. There is also a big non game-related technical part and a preproduction phase behind every game. You will also learn some basic enemy behavior.

Chapter 6, Physics, Qualifiers, and Implementing a Soundtrack, helps you learn about the use of qualifiers when working with many different objects of the same type, such as enemies, weapons, or plants. To make your games scream, you will implement sounds and music in this chapter. We will even take a look at the basics of Fusion's physics!

Chapter 7, Creating Loops and Saving Games, will help you to learn to build a game from the start screen to the result screen, including one of your already created game prototypes. You will also learn how to load and save statistics in your game with the INI object. Global values and simple fast loops will also be covered in this chapter.

Chapter 8, Exporters of Fusion and Mobile Development, will help you learn the basics of developing applications for mobile devices. You have already exported some of your prototypes as a standalone executable file. Now it's time to get to know the other export possibilities of Fusion.

What you need for this book

You will be working with the tool Fusion 2.5 by Clickteam. Fusion is the direct follow-up to the game and application development tool, Clickteam Fusion 2. A lot of tutorials and examples of this book can also be done in Clickteam Fusion 2, which still is a fantastic tool to create 2D games!

Additionally you could use a picture editor of your choice (such as Gimp or Photoshop).

Who this book is for

This book is for game enthusiasts who want to create their own 2D video games but never had the time or the passion or both to learn a scripting language.

Conventions

In this book, you will find a number of styles of text that distinguish between different kinds of information. Here are some examples of these styles, and an explanation of their meaning.

Code words in text are shown as follows: "Open the event editor and look for your old condition: `On collision between bullet and crate`."

A block of code is set as follows:

```
When Button 2 is pressed AND the player is facing to direction 0
Launch the bullet to the right with a speed of 100.
```

New terms and **important words** are shown in bold. Words that you see on the screen, in menus, or dialog boxes for example, appear in the text like this: "Right-click on the already existing condition **Press fire 2** and select **Insert**."

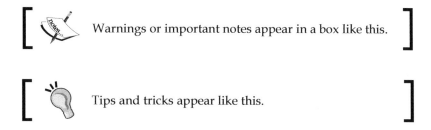

Warnings or important notes appear in a box like this.

Tips and tricks appear like this.

Reader feedback

Feedback from our readers is always welcome. Let us know what you think about this book—what you liked or may have disliked. Reader feedback is important for us to develop titles that you really get the most out of.

To send us general feedback, simply send an e-mail to `feedback@packtpub.com`, and mention the book title via the subject of your message.

If there is a topic that you have expertise in and you are interested in either writing or contributing to a book, see our author guide on `www.packtpub.com/authors`.

Customer support

Now that you are the proud owner of a Packt book, we have a number of things to help you to get the most from your purchase.

Downloading the example code

You can download the example code files for all Packt books you have purchased from your account at http://www.packtpub.com. If you purchased this book elsewhere, you can visit http://www.packtpub.com/support and register to have the files e-mailed directly to you.

Errata

Although we have taken every care to ensure the accuracy of our content, mistakes do happen. If you find a mistake in one of our books—maybe a mistake in the text or the code—we would be grateful if you would report this to us. By doing so, you can save other readers from frustration and help us improve subsequent versions of this book. If you find any errata, please report them by visiting http://www.packtpub.com/submit-errata, selecting your book, clicking on the **errata submission form** link, and entering the details of your errata. Once your errata are verified, your submission will be accepted and the errata will be uploaded on our website, or added to any list of existing errata, under the Errata section of that title. Any existing errata can be viewed by selecting your title from http://www.packtpub.com/support.

Piracy

Piracy of copyright material on the Internet is an ongoing problem across all media. At Packt, we take the protection of our copyright and licenses very seriously. If you come across any illegal copies of our works, in any form, on the Internet, please provide us with the location address or website name immediately so that we can pursue a remedy.

Please contact us at copyright@packtpub.com with a link to the suspected pirated material.

We appreciate your help in protecting our authors, and our ability to bring you valuable content.

Questions

You can contact us at questions@packtpub.com if you are having a problem with any aspect of the book, and we will do our best to address it.

1
The Basics of Fusion

In this chapter, we will cover the following points:

- Creating a video game
- The basics of the Fusion user interface
- Getting started

Learning a new tool is a challenging task. This chapter will introduce you to the world of game development with Fusion by Clickteam. You'll learn the basics of the tools' user interface and how to begin developing games.

About creating a video game

You want to create video games, and that is awesome! It's as simple as that! Welcome to the circle of game developers! I don't know where your motivation comes from. Maybe your older brother introduced you to video games and you fell in love. Maybe you already are a passionate player. Maybe you just found out about this cool art form or you've always wanted to create your own game, but you just never knew how or where to start. Whatever your reasons are—you are in the exact right place— at the exact right time. I will try my best to assist you in making your dream come true with Fusion!

So let's start with the main question: What is necessary to create a video game?

Well, you obviously own a game development tool if you are reading this book. That's something we can start with! But what I mean is what ingredients do we need to create a game?

There might be some simple steps that we may have to follow when we want to create a game. Nothing can be simpler than that, I guess!

Let's pick a genre first. That might be a good start. This shouldn't be too hard—there are only a couple of genres out there. Platformers, top-down shooter, or RPGs are very common, right?

Think about some cute graphics. Or maybe you want to create a game for a more grown-up audience. Well, in that case, just use some cool, tech, spacey graphics!

What else… let's see… characters of course! We need a likable anti-hero. Or at least a heroic spaceship—armed to the teeth! Let's add some special features you want to see in your game, such as low gravity or a teleportation gun. Be creative! Surprise us!

Some people might call these features the **unique selling proposition (USP)**. So think of what makes your game different? Why should we play your game? This sounds simple, but after so many years of video games, it is actually very hard to invent new features or even better, a new genre!

When it comes to ,music and sound effects…please do not make the mistake that so many developers do of forgetting the impact and importance of a good soundtrack. Just think of that one game you really love. What happens to you when you hear the title song? What are you feeling? I know it might be hard to describe, and maybe that's exactly the reason why you should really think of the sound effects and the music of your game. I'm sure you want to create that special moment for every single player out there! The following link would be a perfect example for one of my favorite games:

`http://www.youtube.com/watch?v=Ye5TV9pa_4Y&feature=share`

So what have we got? We have the genre, cool graphics, sweet characters or a heroic battleship, awesome features, and a fantastic soundtrack. Did we forget something? Well, what about the idea? The game idea itself!

Never underestimate the idea! There are tons of first person shooters, millions of car or racing games, and thousands of platformers. All great ideas will be cloned and remade sooner or later.

My friends and I have paid homage to a couple of our favorite Jump 'n' Runs with **Pitiri** 1977. But like so many before and aside us, we did not quite reach that level of "Wow!". Oh, that's what I'm going to call it from now on: the level of Wow!

An idea (I might quote a ton of movies and quite a lot of poets at this point) can be more powerful than a million copies of something. Of course, selling a million copies of that very idea can be pretty sweet too, but that's another story. We do not want to make a lot of money in the first place; we want to create a lot of great games, right?

If you have a good idea, work on it. Tweak it. Play around with it until you have that feeling. When you are quite satisfied—show your ideas to others. I would start with close and honest friends. Show it to people who will tell you right away if something is a good idea or a bad one—if something is boring or a great new game! Maybe you are the one with the next breakthrough game!

Getting to know some terms about the tool

Fusion (followup to Clickteam Fusion 2) is a tool that allows you to create all kinds of games, applications, programs, and even old-school screensavers! And all that without any knowledge of a programming language! Of course, there are some terms that you should know about before we go straight to our first game!

The application

Fusion creates applications. Call them apps, games, or presentations. Everything you create will be saved as an application with the extension .mfa on your hard drive.

The frames

Frames correspond to the different screens of your application. They can be levels of a game, sites of a homepage, slides in a multimedia presentation, and so on. Let's take a simple game as an example: the first frame would be the splash screen, the second frame would be the game itself, and the third frame would be the high-score table!

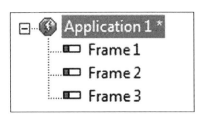

The objects

Objects are dropped in a frame. They are the different *actors* of your application. Fusion contains a lot of different objects to suit different tasks. For example, an **Active** object can be used as a character in a game; a **String** object can display some text, such as a score; the **Accelerometer** object reads useable data from the gyro sensor of a mobile phone; and so on. Objects are dropped on the frame in the frame editor. Each object can also have a number of conditions, actions, and expressions to control and define how they act while the application is running. The following screenshot shows different types of objects:

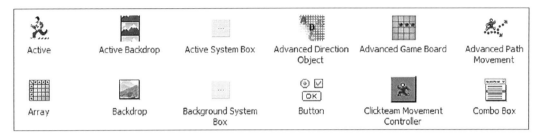

The properties

All objects are defined by their set of properties found in the properties toolbar. Properties consist of adjustable values (texts, options, colors, fonts, and so on) that precisely define your objects' behavior. Just like every object, frames also have customizable properties that define how your application will act when run. The following screenshot shows the **Properties** toolbar:

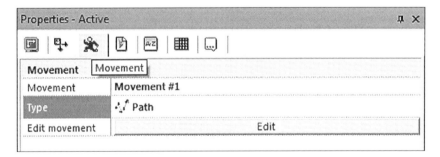

The events

The logic of your application is defined with events. Events will control everything about your objects, such as whether your object should move, play an animation, perform calculations, or be destroyed. You can call the events (and the event editor) "The heart of Fusion"; sounds very epic, doesn't it?

Events—and this is the important part—are the way to program any and all applications in Fusion! You enter and edit the events in the event editor. Events are made of **conditions** and **actions**.

Conditions and actions

Conditions are simple questions that can be true or false.

Upon pressing "J" is be a condition, as you can see in the following screenshot:

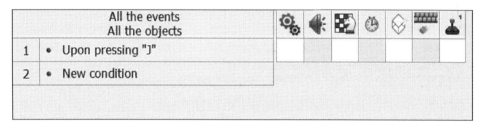

This condition will be set to true if the player presses the key *J* while the application is running. An event can contain more than one condition, each listed after the other. If the first condition is met, Fusion immediately checks to see whether the next conditions are met in descending order. For the event to be considered true, all of the events must be true at the same time. When the conditions of an event are true, the actions of the event are executed.

An action is a task to perform when the conditions are true. *Add 10 to score of player 1* can be our action.

When this action is run, 10 points are added to the score of player 1. An event can also contain more than one action; in that case, they will be executed one after the other.

Combine the condition with the action and you get your first event as **Upon pressing "J"** — add 10 to score of player 1:

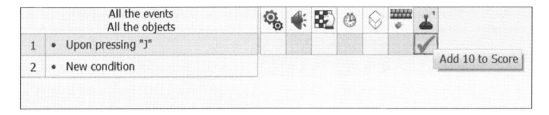

It's as simple as that! You will work with a lot of those **If... then** events during your development process.

The basics of the Fusion user interface

As you will see, the interface of every editor in Fusion is built in a similar, very intuitive way. Too many toolbars would be confusing. Fusion reduces the number to a minimum:

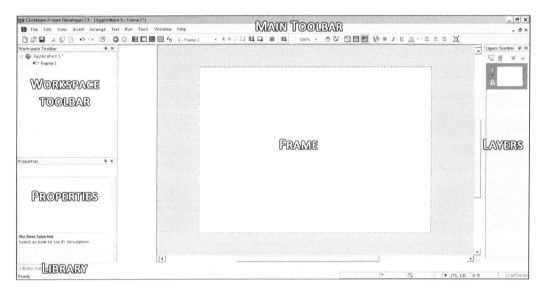

The top section

The main toolbar lets you navigate through Fusion and its editors. Of course, it also includes the standard application elements (new, save, load, and so on), and it also has some options to help with your workspace management. But I really think you will find out about all the options by yourself with time.

The left section

The **Workspace Toolbar** includes your opened applications (games) and all its frames. This is your main window to manage the frames of your game and switch from scene to scene!

The **Properties** window will show all the properties depending on which object or frame is selected.

The center section

The frame is where all the action takes place. This is where all your little characters, spaceships, and squirrels (yes, squirrels!) will play around. It's the stage for your protagonists.

The right section

Add and edit your layers on the right-hand side of the screen. Arrange all your objects on different layers and use layer-specific effects such as parallax scrolling.

The bottom section

Use **Library Toolbar** on the bottom-left side to import assets from your library. Your current objects stats, such as size or position, can be viewed on the bottom-right of the screen:

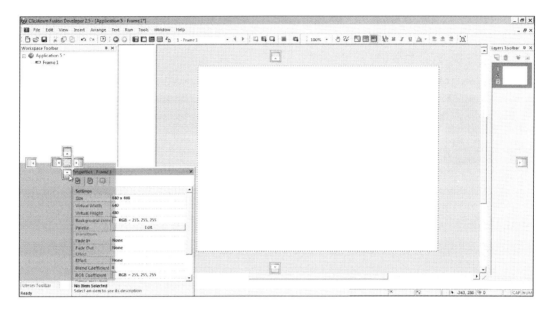

All the toolbars and windows can be arranged as you like. Just drag the single panels from one place to another to personalize your screen.

Getting to know the interface of Fusion might take some time. But you will soon realize that it is structured very intuitively. For detailed instructions of every icon in the toolbar, use the built-in help file (press *F1*) that includes every little option and button you might find somewhere around Fusion.

Getting started

At the moment, we need to start somewhere. As a starter, you should begin small, and pretty soon—I am sure about that—you will slowly develop your dream games! These next steps are just little guidelines to simplify the very beginning:

1. **Brainstorming**: Pick one of your favorite arcade games that was made before 1980 and try to build some pieces of that game using events.

2. **Prototyping**: Take what you have learned and try to modify the cloned game mechanics to make them more interesting, or start prototyping the mechanics of your most simple game idea.

3. **Greenlight**: Share your prototype game mechanics with your friends, family, and the online Fusion community. They can all give you feedback and ideas on how to make your game even better.

4. **Alpha**: Transform your prototype mechanics into a real game, with goals, rules, and lots of fun!

5. **Closed Beta**: Release your game as a Beta, and let people play through it from start to finish so that they can give you even more feedback on how to make it awesome.

6. **Open Beta**: Fix bugs and glitches; balance the gameplay; upgrade the art, and polish, polish, polish! Get your game into a state where you are happy with it and where people who play your game will want to share it with their friends.

7. **Gold Master**: Throw a launch party and release your game into the wild for everyone to enjoy your hard work. Be proud of what you've made! This sounds way easier than it is. All of my friends who tend to be game developers have at least a dozen abandoned projects in their development graveyard. That's a shame because a lot of those ideas had some great potential! So at the risk of repeating myself: don't give up. I know you can finish your game.

Now it's time to jump in. Boot up your copy of Fusion and let's start making your first game!

Summary

You have learned the basics of Fusion's interface. You know how to operate the tool and where to find the most important properties and options. You have also read a brief overview of game development and design. Now you are ready to start your very first game project using Fusion. *Chapter 2, The Editors of Fusion – Your First Game!*, will show you how to work with the editors of Fusion to create your first game prototype.

2
The Editors of Fusion – Your First Game!

Everything in Fusion is constructed to be very intuitive and easy to learn. However, it takes some time to understand the mechanics of the tool. This chapter will give you an overview of the different editors and their usage.

In this chapter, we will cover:

- The editors – an overview
- The frame editor
- The picture and animation editors
- The event editor

The editors – an overview

It would take too long to describe *everything* you will encounter during your first hours with Fusion. I can only lead you through your first prototypes. However, just in case you are curious and want to learn more steps, there is an excellent help file that includes descriptions of every single button and area of the tool. Just hit *F1* in Fusion.

Opening and navigating through the main editors

To open the storyboard, frame, and event editors, you usually select the application or frame to edit in the workspace window or in the storyboard editor. Then, you either click on one of the editor buttons in the navigate toolbar or right-click on the item and select an edit command in the context menu.

Clickteam Fusion 2.5 opens one frame window per application. When you open an editor, it will be opened in this window, replacing the previous one. For example, if you open the storyboard editor and then edit a frame, the frame editor will replace the storyboard editor in the same window. You can navigate through the previously opened editors with the red Back/Forward buttons.

Here is a little overview about the editors you will use in the next chapters:

1. After you have created a new application, you'll enter the storyboard editor. You will always get a perfect overview of your games levels (frames) there. An application (the full game) generally consists of several frames (the levels, menus, screens, and so on).

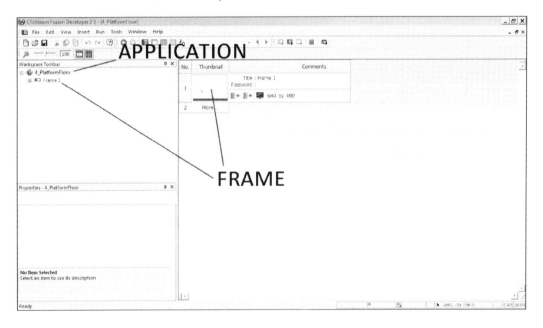

Each of the frames in your application will be edited in the frame editor. You will start with only one frame. Open it by double-clicking on **Frame 1**. You will spend half of your time in Fusion with creating levels and the layout of your game.

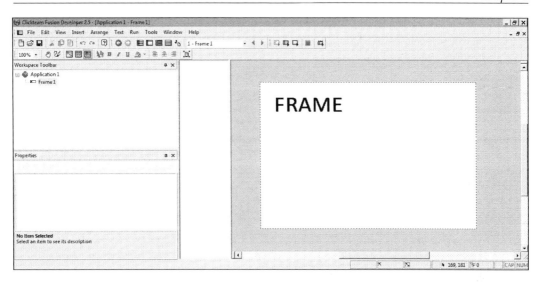

2. Right-click anywhere in your frame and select **Insert object**. In the open window, select **Active** and click on **Ok**. Double-clicking on any graphical object (like the created active object) will open up the picture editor. Create your own pixel art graphics or import external art files and work with them in this editor. The **Animations** section at the bottom of the editor allows you to define animation sets for your objects; all you need to do is define the order and speed at which the frames will be displayed.

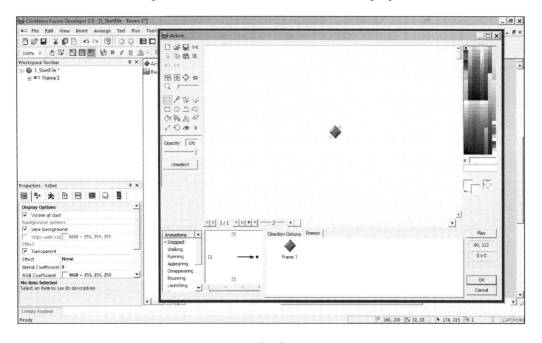

3. Now open the event editor by clicking on the Event Editor icon in the toolbar at the top of the screen.

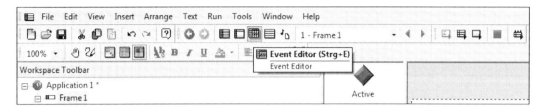

All the programming will happen in the event editor. This is where you will spend the other half of your time! Create all your events, conditions, and actions in a perfectly clear spreadsheet system. You will learn how to create and use events in the next section of this chapter. Consider the following screenshot:

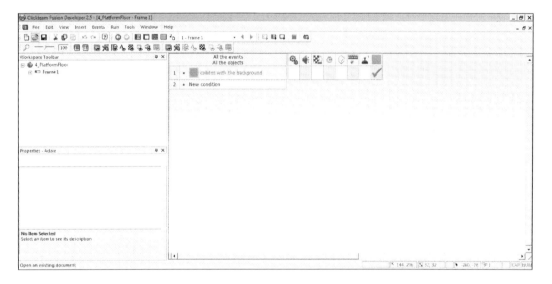

4. All calculations are edited in the expression editor. If you want to change the running speed of your main character or change the color of the background to neon pink, then all these steps will be processed in the expression editor. You'll learn the straightforward functioning of the expression editor in the next section of this chapter. Consider the following screenshot:

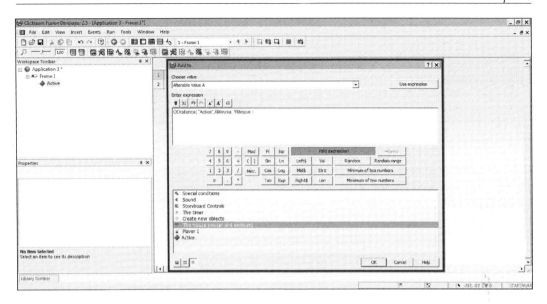

The frame editor

This book will not describe every little bit and piece of Fusion, but it will lead you through this powerful tool to create your first own game!

For now, let's create a new application, shall we?

Create a new application by clicking on the New icon in the top-left corner of the toolbar. Then, go straight to Frame 1 by double-clicking on the white rectangle or the label **Frame 1**.

What you are seeing now is the frame editor, which is one of the most important editors in Fusion. It allows you to pose all of the objects within the currently selected frame of the application.

Let's create an active object by double-clicking somewhere on your frame in the center of the screen. A new window appears containing all the possible extensions and objects you can choose to create.

Now choose the object **Active** and place it wherever you want in within your frame.

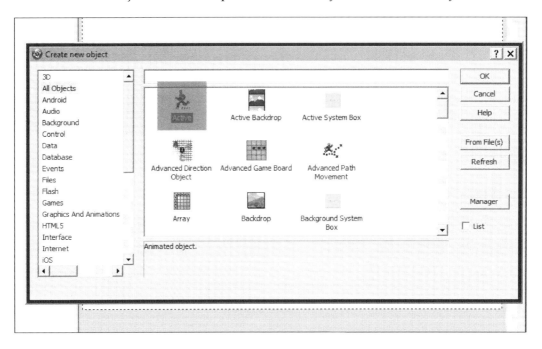

Congratulations! You have just created your first game object! Now select the active object and look at the properties to the lower-left corner of your screen. This is where you can change the properties of your active object. For now, select the **Movement** tab and click on the Static icon beside **Type**. The screen that appears shows the built-in movement possibilities of Fusion. Active objects can be set to all kinds of built-in movements such as platform movement or eight direction movement. These movements will automatically turn your former static object to a controllable, moving object! You will learn about the most common movements in the following chapters.

Select the **Platform** movement in the non-physical movements section.

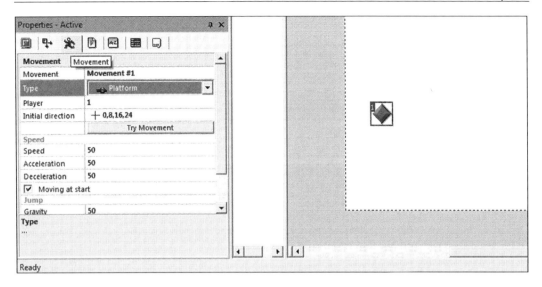

I guess you now know what our first game prototype will be! Yes, exactly! It's going to be a little Jump 'n' Run! Woohoo! It's time to get to know some of the properties of the active object.

Fool around with **Speed**, **Acceleration**, **Deceleration**, and so forth. There are no right or wrong values for these settings. It always depends on the desired feel for the controls of your characters. For example, if your game takes place in space, you might want to play around with adjusting the gravity setting or your characters, or if your main character is a grandmother, you may want to have a low speed value.

Hit *F7* to start this frame (this level of your game). You will also find the **Run Frame** option in the header bar of Fusion on the top of the screen. *F7* will always start your current frame (level). If you want to start the complete application from top to toe, hit *F8*. This, of course, will be much more interesting and will be covered in the upcoming chapters!

What's happening? Your little active object is falling down. Gravity is doing its job. We have to place a floor that your character can walk on!

Double-click somewhere in the frame and then create a new **Backdrop** object. Backdrop objects are very powerful when creating simple games such as platformers because you can make them an obstacle type. This means they will automatically have a solid collision between themselves and your active object, making them perfect for floors, walls, and any other simple obstacle you need.

It's time to save your application. This is something I would recommend you do as often as possible. Create new save copies every now and then—do not always overwrite one single file. Plenty of disc space is available these days. Save your application by navigating to **File | Save As**. Choose a filename and hit **Save**. As you want to save *as often as possible*, choose a filename such as Applicationname_01, so you can always keep track of the version number of your application. It's often simple tricks such as these that will make your life as a game developer much easier!

The picture and animation editor

There are many tools to create or manipulate game graphics, such as Photoshop, Gimp, and Pixelmator. Regardless of your image editing preference, you will end up using the picture and animation editor in Fusion. This editor is not only the most central editor for all your graphics, but it is also used to adjust how all objects move in relation to their animation frames and even to create reference spots on your objects, such as a head or gun barrel.

The picture editor will open automatically when you double-click on any object, so go ahead and double-click on your active backdrop object. Consider the following screenshot:

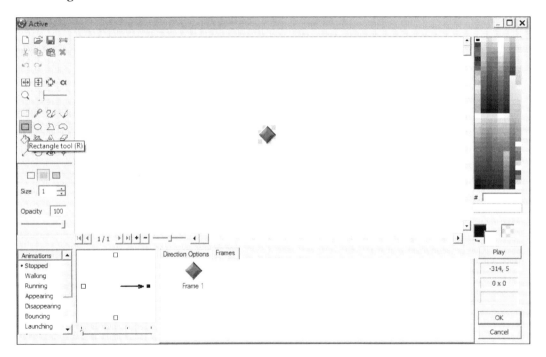

In the top-left corner, you see all the available tools such as the Brush or Rectangle tool. The right-hand side shows all the beautiful colors you can use! The animation editor can be found at the bottom of this window. We will work with all those options later. For now, let's stick with some simple design tools to create your first platformer object.

Choose the Rectangle tool (see the preceding screenshot) and set it to **filled** in the rectangle options below. Choose any color you prefer from the color squares on the right-hand side. You can also pick a color with the color picker tool. You can fool around with the tools if you want.

What we will do now is to set the hot spot and the action point of our square character. Select the hot spot tool (the little eye in your tools on the left-hand side of the screen). The hot spot defines the actual center of your object. All the references to this object anywhere in the game will treat the center of the object as this spot. It will rotate around this spot or attach other objects to this very spot if you want to. This is a very important feature and will be used throughout your future games.

If the hot spot is your object's point of reference for the world, then the action point is other objects' point of reference for that object. For example, an action point can be the location where you want special effects or other objects to appear (afterburners, muzzle flashes, or where to stick a hat). Like the hot spot, the action point always sticks with your object if it moves. Select it by clicking on the star icon next to the hot spot eye.

For now, place the hot spot in the center of your graphic by clicking on the center square of the nine small quick move fields. Use the quick move fields again to place the action point to the right-hand side of your active object.

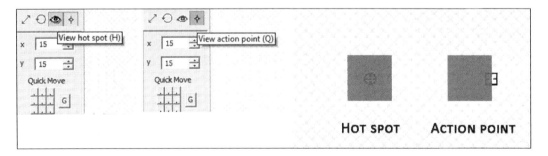

Look at the following screenshot of the animation editor. You can see that we are presently looking at our character in the **Stopped** animation. The next window displays which direction our character is facing, which in this case is the right. The last section shows each individual frame of animation (for our character and this tutorial, we will only have one frame). Our platforming character will want to be able to face right and left, so click on the tiny white box on the left to show what our character would look like while facing left for the **Stopped** animation. You'll notice nothing appears in the **Frames** tab. Go back to viewing our character while facing right, select that frame (**Frame 1**), and copy (*Ctrl + C*) it. Then go back to viewing our character while facing left and paste (*Ctrl + V*) the frame there.

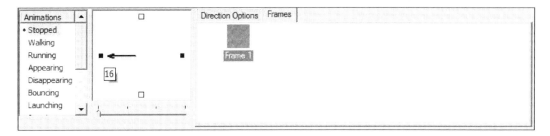

The last thing you have to do now is flip your character so that it looks left when it is facing left. Right-click on your graphic in the image editing window and select **Flip horizontally**. This will automatically flip all your selected objects (if you have more) in the opposite direction. This will flip your object (including the hot spot and action point) to the left-hand side. Now open the backdrop and use what you have just learned to create a brownish square. Just use your imagination! Click on **Ok** after you are done applying your changes.

Right-click on the backdrop object. An **Option** window will pop up.

Selecting the **Create** option on an object will turn either an active object to a backdrop or the other way round.

We want to create a so-called quick backdrop. The difference between this and a standard backdrop is that you can easily create huge tiled areas with quick backdrops, which can be useful for floors or backgrounds.

What you will get is a 100 square tiled version of your old backdrop. Scale this square to any size you like. You can either scale the quick backdrop in the properties window or directly scale the object within the frame. Click on the object once. Little black squares will appear in each corner and on all four sides. Drag one of those squares in any direction to scale the object!

In our case, a 640 x 32 big quick backdrop will do a great job as a simple floor. This is how you create a simple floor with only one single 32 x 32 pixel square! The properties should already be set to **obstacle**. If not, do so and of course feel free to fool around with all the other options of the quick backdrop object. Last but not least, move the created floor below the player object.

The event editor

We want to stop our player when they collide with a backdrop—our floor. To create this effect, open the event editor. The first row and column has the words **New Condition** listed. This is where you define something for the game to check (condition) in order to make something happen (action). Consider the following code snippet:

```
New condition
```

Downloading the example code

You can download the example code files for all Packt books you have purchased from your account at http://www.packtpub.com. If you purchased this book elsewhere, you can visit http://www.packtpub.com/ support and register to have the files e-mailed directly to you.

Click on it and a new window showing all of your game objects will appear. In the event editor menus, all you usually need to do is click once to select the desired object or effect and the menu will do the rest. Choose your active object and remember that is your character. Navigate to **Collision | backdrop**. You have successfully created the condition: Player collides with the background.

Now you will have to choose an action for this collision. You want your character to be stopped by the floor. Right-click on the column of your player object for this event and navigate to **Movement | Stop**. This is your first action. Condition and action combined make your first event, which looks like this:

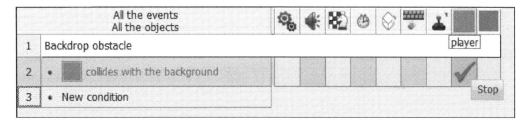

The procedure for events will always be the same. You select a condition in the left-hand column and add the appropriate action under the required object on one of the right-hand columns. You can add as many actions as you like if you want more actions to occur.

Your character is all set to interact with the floor. Hit *F7* and test your level! You can move your character with the arrow keys and jump with *Shift* (button 1).

If not already done, go back to the properties of your player and tweak the settings until your character's movement feels right. That is a very important part of the whole game creating process.

How does the movement feel? Think of your game's setting again. Are we on earth or in space with low gravity? Are we on solid ground or underwater? Create the world of your game in your head. Each adjustment to a property value can have a big impact on the feel of your game. We will work on exactly how these properties impact the feel of your game later in these tutorials, but feel free to make simple adjustments now just to see how they act on your character. Be sure to set them back close to default before moving on. You will get a feel for it after a couple of prototypes.

Obstacles

Time to place some obstacles within your game world. Let's call it some initial steps in level design!

Create another backdrop object. Open the picture editor and select the Rectangle tool again. Draw a simple square and click on **Ok**. You will get a 32 x 32 pixel square. Set **obstacle type** to **obstacle** in properties again and you're all set. Place this block anywhere in your level and the collision event with the player and backdrops created for the floor will also affect this box.

Basically, you have got all you need to create a basic platformer stage. You've got the floor, the player, and a simple obstacle square. To create a level, you might want to duplicate the obstacle a couple of times to create something like an environment. Do so by dragging as many obstacles as you like from the Object list (see the following screenshot) and arranging it within your newly created level. Your frame may look a bit like this now:

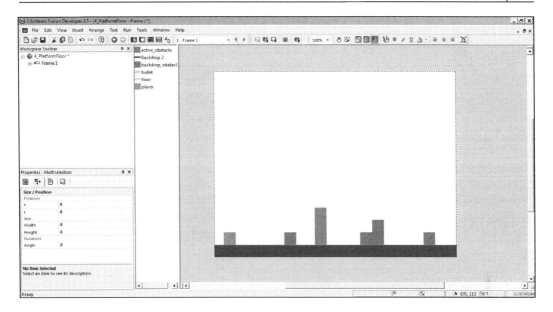

Now go to the event editor and create the following condition from the special conditions (the two gears):

```
Collision between "Player" and "Obstacle"
```

Downloading the example code

You can download the example code files for all Packt books you have purchased from your account at http://www.packtpub.com. If you purchased this book elsewhere, you can visit http://www.packtpub.com/support and register to have the files e-mailed directly to you.

Select the player object and again navigate to **Movement | Stop**. You can also just drag the action **Movement | Stop** from event created before to your new condition!

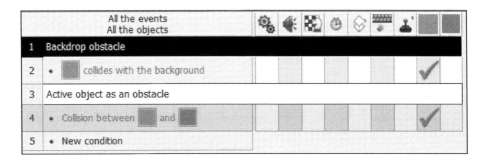

Naming

Just one more hint before we go on. Try to name and comment as much as possible. Name your character `player`, your backdrops `blocks`, and you're your floor. Comment your events in the event editor by inserting comments every now and then (right-click on the numbers at the very tip of every condition and insert a comment). All of this is very important, because though your game might look empty and clear now, it will grow and flourish, and after a while you will be happy about every single comment and every well named object.

Scrolling

By now, you should have built a simple level. But what if your player leaves the play area on any of the sides? You need some kind of automated camera that follows your character. You need scrolling!

Scrolling is one of the most essential camera logics for platformers and video games in general. A basic scrolling technique can be done with only one line in Fusion.

Visit the event editor again. Choose the condition **Always** and select **Scrollings | Center window position in frame** from Storyboard Controls. You'll be asked to select your scrolling object—the player.

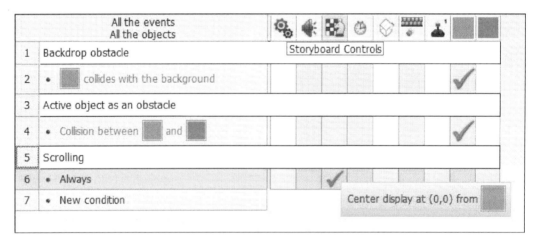

Of course, the level (in our case, the frame) needs to be extended. Go back to the frame editor and select **Frame 1** in the workspace toolbar to the left. Now go down to its properties and change **Size** from **640 x 480** to **1200 x 480**. This means that the length of your level is 1200 pixels now.

Ignore the virtual width and height for now. Your game area will expand and you'll instantly have more space for more cool stuff! The game area can theoretically be sized up to a billion, but of course the frame size will affect the performance.

Like in previous steps, feel free to play around with the properties of Frame 1. Don't forget to also extend your floor to the size of 1200. Just scale up your floor backdrop to the desired size in its properties. Then hit *F7* and enjoy your first designed level!

Shoot 'em up!

Of course, your character needs opponents. That is something like a law of physics. Of course, your character has to cope up with that opponent in some way. The classic would be a Mario-like "jump on that Goomba!" attack. We want to use another classic for our prototype though: a simple "Shoot 'Em Up" attack such as in the old Contra, Turrican, or Metal Slug games. We will get to enemy movement and **artificial intelligence (AI)** later. But for now, we just want to learn how to launch an object from our player!

Create an active object and paint a bullet. Also set the hot spot and the action point to the center of your bullet. I'm sure you've been playing around with the tools in Fusion's picture editor already, but one of the most important tools is the Crop tool (*Ctrl + K*).

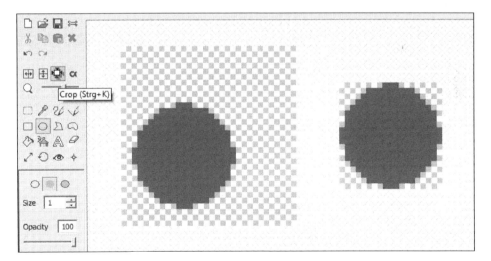

Hitting the crop button will crop all the unused space outside your object, right to the borders of your graphic. You will use this method a million times from now on. You are allowed to open your mind, let your spirit fly, and get creative while working on your bullet's style now! Surprise us with fireballs, laser beams, plasma arrows, or whatever fits in your game!

Open the event editor and navigate to **Joystick | Read Joystick state**. Then select **Button 2** and unselect **Up arrow**, which is selected by default. Remember, button 1 is your jump button. So your condition would be as follows:

```
Press Fire Button 2
```

As an action, you'll choose your player object. Select **Launch an Object**. Choose your recently created bullet and click on **Ok**. A window will pop up. Choose **Launch in selected directions...** and select the direction **0** (right). Don't forget to unselect the direction **8** (up). This means that your character will launch a bullet to the right with a speed of 100 whenever you hit button 2 (*Ctrl*)!

Your event editor should look something like this now:

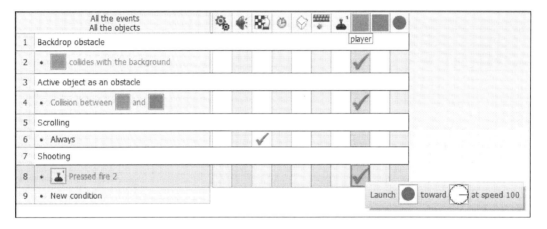

When you test your game, you'll see that the character will always fire the bullet to the right. What we want though is that he shoots left and right, depending on the player's direction. So we're going to add one more condition to the already existing event.

Right-click on the already existing condition **Press fire 2** and select **Insert**. Now choose your character and navigate to **Direction | Compare direction of player**. An arrow to the 0 (right) should be set by default. Leave it that way. What we have done here is combine two conditions into a single, more precise state. This is something you will use a lot from now on. Consider the following condition:

```
When Button 2 is pressed AND the player is facing to direction 0
Launch the bullet to the right with a speed of 100.
```

The only thing that's left is the other direction. Duplicate the last event. Now set the player's direction in the condition to left. Repeat the same procedure with the bullet direction:

```
When Button 2 is pressed AND the player is facing to direction 16
Launch the bullet to the left with a speed of 100.
```

Your player will shoot left and right, depending on your character's direction! Well done!

Now you will also understand why we have placed the hot spot and the action point in the first place. Your character rotates left and right perfectly from its center, but shoots from its action point at the character's side.

Summary

You have made a huge step towards game development with this chapter. You have basically learned how to create a simple platform shooter! You have been introduced to the main editors of Fusion and how those editors fundamentally work. So here comes the good news: this is actually how everything in Fusion works!

Of course, things will get more and more complex from now on. But in general, this system of creating objects, adding behaviors, changing properties or style, and combining all those parts as one will be repeated over and over again.

The next chapter will teach you everything about Fusion's extension and object system. You will also learn more about animations and colliders in Fusion.

3
Movements, Animations, and Graphics

This chapter is all about movement and how to breathe life into your game. You'll also learn the basics of animations and the animation editor. As well as this, you'll also learn about the types of built-in movement, which are one of the most essential benefits of Fusion. In this chapter, we will cover:

- Creating animations
- Simple particles
- Clickteam movements
- Importing graphics and animations
- Working with layers

Creating animations – how to blow up crates!

It's time to test your bullets on something! For that reason, you will create a simple, active object. Feel free to draw a little wooden or metal crate—anything you've always wanted to blow to pieces.

The animation editor is placed in the bottom section of the picture editor that you have already used to create simple, non-animated graphics. Every active object can have a number of animations, and these animations are used when the object is moving on the screen. Each active object can have an unlimited number of animations. There are several default animations with names ranging from **Stopped** to **Stand Up**, but you can add as many additional animations with custom names as you'd like. Be careful when using the default animations because different Fusion movement types and events will trigger certain default animations automatically.

We will use the **Disappearing** preset for our exploding crate. Fusion will automatically play the disappearing animation when your object is destroyed.

For now, copy your "stopped crate" graphic and paste it to the first frame of the disappearing slot. Now copy and paste the same crate to create a second frame for the disappearing animation. Try to destroy your crate a bit. For example, you could use the eraser tool to delete some parts of your crate. Then copy and paste this slightly destroyed crate to frame 3, and erase a bit more. Repeat this step as often as you like to create your first animation.

If you need more space for one of your graphics, just click on the Size tool, and enlarge the picture area as shown in the following screenshot:

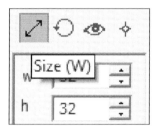

To change the speed of your animation, go to the **Direction Options** tab, and set the animation speed to the value of your choice. You can click on the **Play** button near the bottom right of the image editor to preview your animation and make sure the playback speed is appropriate. Of course, you have to test your animations during runtime to find out the right speed. Consider the following screenshot:

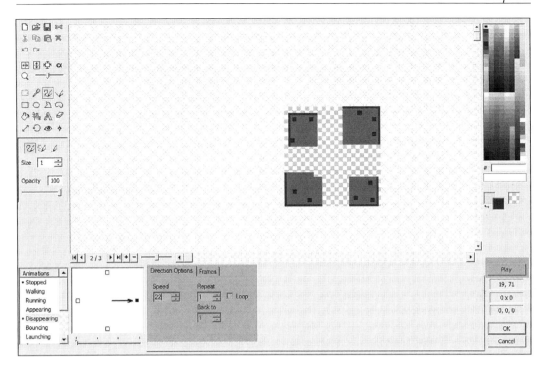

A simple rule for animations in Fusion: the more pictures you have in one animation section, the more fluid your animation will be. The downside is that the animation takes longer to play, so it might make the controls feel sluggish or less responsive. In general, I use four to six frames for simple pixel games. For some more complex games with hand-painted graphics, I use 10 to 12 frames. In the end, it depends on your style, the desired file size, the way you want your game to look and feel, and of course the time you can spend on painting!

To sum it up: you should just have created a simple crate graphic in the **Stopped** section and the crate-pieces animation in the **Disappearing** section. The speed of your animation has been set too. Now you have to write an event that will tell the crate to be destroyed when hit by a bullet. Go to the event editor and create the following condition:

```
On collision between bullet and crate
```

This condition will trigger the following two actions:

```
Destroy bullet & Destroy crate
```

You could also include your backdrops or obstacles to this condition. The bullet will be destroyed if it touches your environment. If you hit *F7* to test your frame, you will realize that your crate will explode when you hit it with one of your bullets!

Simple particles

Now let's add some nice and simple particles to this crate explosion. We want a couple of little boxes to explode from the crate and bounce a bit before they are destroyed themselves. To produce this effect, create a new active object; draw just a small particle in the color of your crate and duplicate it four times within your **Stopped** animation. Set **Speed** of this animation to 4, and close the picture editor.

You will now learn a bit about the next Clickteam movement. Go to the properties of your crate particle, and select **Pinball movement** from the **Movement** extensions selection.

The **Pinball movement** makes your active object move like a pinball—a bouncing ball with gravity. That is exactly what we want for our simple particles! Set **Gravity** to 12 and **Initial speed** to 30. Also set **Initial direction** to 6 to 8 of the top arrows. This defines the direction of the object when the movement starts or the object has been created. If you choose more than one direction, a random direction within the selected ones will be chosen. In our case, the particle will bounce up with the initial speed of 30 and a gravity of 12, which will drag the object down after a while.

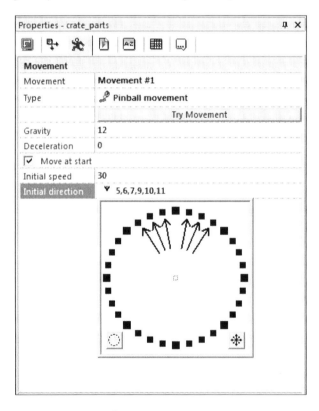

Open the event editor and look for your old condition: `On collision between bullet and crate`. Go to the fourth column (create objects), and select **Create object**. Search for your particle, select it, and choose **Relative to crate** when the next pop up appears. This will create one particle relative to your crate when it gets hit by a bullet. Duplicate the same action (create particle relative to crate) in the very same place six times to create six particles when the event takes place.

Create a new condition, and set **Movement** of your particle to **Bounce** when it collides with a backdrop (your floor and your obstacles). As your final condition, go to your particle and look for animation. Select the condition: `Compare current frame of particle to a value`. The window that appears is the expression editor. This editor appears when you need to enter a value for an action or a condition. The expression editor works like an advanced calculator. The current expression is displayed in the white edit zone and you can click on any of the buttons to enter a new value.

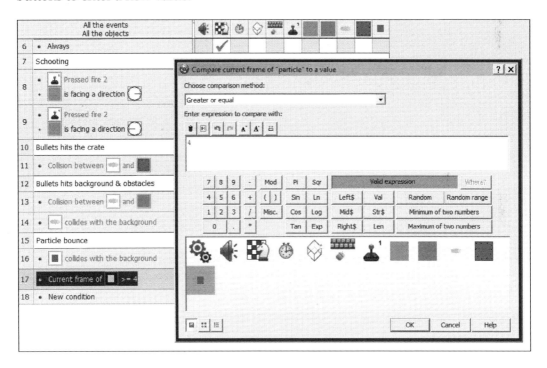

We want to create a very simple calculation that destroys our particle object when the animation reaches frame 4 or higher. Remember, you have duplicated your particle graphic four times and, therefore, created a five frame animation. Consider the following condition:

```
If current frame of particle >= 4 then destroy particle
```

You can choose different states when working with the expression editor: equal, different, greater/lower, and greater/lower/equal. So you can check whether your animation is below, equal to, or higher than, a specific value.

Press *F7* and test your new events. The crate will change to the **Disappearing** animation when it collides with a bullet. Additionally six particles will appear at the destroyed crates position and bounce on the floor until its animations reach frame 4.

Clickteam movements

You have already used two different built-in movements, the simple platform and the pinball movement in *Chapter 2, The Editors of Fusion – Your First Game!*. Both are very helpful for creating small games or prototypes, but there are many more built-in movements you can choose from.

All the movements are controlled by keyboard, mouse, or a joypad/joystick when you are working on a personal computer. There is a default setting for both input devices (depending on which you want to use). Change this default input in the application properties, under **Default Controls**, in the **Runtime options** tab. You can easily select any key or button as your new default input as shown in the following screenshot:

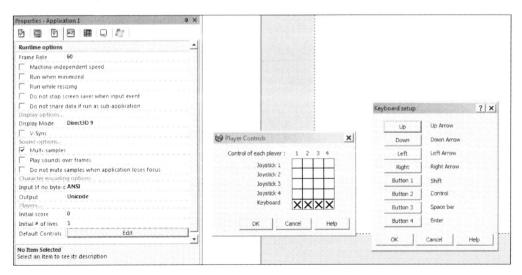

As you can see, you can set up the controls for up to four players. You could, for example, set the movement controls of player one to the keys *W*, *A*, *S*, *D* and the movement controls of player two to the arrow keys to create a two-player game on one screen.

Non physical movements

In the beginning, we will focus on the non-physical movements, which include some of the most basic and common classic movements of 2D video games. Just select your active object and choose the desired movement in its properties!

The bouncing ball movement

An object with this movement will bounce like a rubber ball on obstacles. This simple movement can be used in a lot of other ways. It can be seen as the motor of an object. It will apply an impulse, but you can decide the direction, the speed, or the dynamic.

You can create a very simple AI when setting the direction of an active object (the enemy) to your player's position and applying the bouncing ball movement. The enemy will now follow your player wherever he moves.

The path movement

The path movement makes your object follow a given path. You can draw or set this path with a few simple clicks. The path movement setup is done via a dialog box, and not via a list of properties. You just have to click on the **Edit** button in the property list to open the dialog box. A path movement is represented as a line made of different segments. Each segment is separated from the other by a node. Select a node to set the speed for the next segment. This allows you to create unlimited little paths with different speeds.

You could use a simple one-path solution for your exploding crate from the platformer example to create a simple enemy. Just place two nodes to create a path. Now activate **Loop the movement** and **Return at end** in the path movement tool box. Your enemy will march on this path till eternity!

The mouse-controlled movement

The mouse movement lets you control an object using the mouse. At runtime, a Windows mouse pointer will disappear and the given object will move accordingly with the mouse. You can also restrict the zone in which the object moves.

I would recommend setting your object to the x and y coefficients of your mouse pointer in the event editor as an alternative though. This creates a simpler and more flexible mouse controlled movement. Create the condition `Always`. Then create the action `x position` of your active object to `Current x position of the mouse`. Repeat the same procedure with the y position and you get a simple mouse movement.

The eight-directions movement

There is a famous eight-direction movement for all you top-down RPG fans out there. It is very easy to handle and powerful in the beginning. You can adjust the acceleration, deceleration, and speed of your object. That's pretty much it.

Race car

This movement might be interesting to you if you want to create a classic top-down racing game. Your active object will have acceleration and deceleration with up and down, and steering with left and right. This movement might be useful when you just want to prototype a little car racing game.

Movement extensions

For now, skip the physical movements, as you will learn more about this exciting topic in a later chapter. This might be hard, as we all know how cool it is to play around with physics, but you will read half a chapter about physics later.

So if you have tested plenty of the non-physical movements, try to fool around with the movement extensions now. These movements are mainly designed for non-player objects. This means that most of those movements will not be controlled by the player and are, therefore, perfect for automated movements.

You have already tested the pinball movement for your particles. The object with this movement will act just like a body with gravity and speed. As you have already experienced, it can not only be used for pinball games, but also for particles. Always remember that the Clickteam movements can be used for whatever you might need them. Just think creatively and don't be afraid to experiment!

The spaceship movement is the only player-controlled movement of this section and might be a bit tricky in the beginning. It can be used to create a basic version of the typical asteroids movement. Create an active object, center the hotspot, and enable **Automatic Rotations** in the object's properties. To test the classic version of this movement, deactivate gravity in the movement properties, and set both **Power of thrust** and **Rotation speed** to `70`.

The remaining movement extensions should be straightforward and easy to understand. Just apply the single movements from **Circular** to **InAndOut** to a dummy active object and see what happens. You will find out about the handling and use of the remaining movement extensions. There is not only one right situation for each of those movements, but as many as you decide to have.

Importing graphics and animations

You may have realized that we have not paid too much attention to the graphics. The game itself always comes first. Yes, style is important, but the root of your game will always be its gameplay and handling. If you are satisfied with the feeling of your prototype, then you can start to think of your games graphics.

It is very simple to import graphics or frame-by-frame animations to different objects in Fusion. You can import graphics to all kind of objects or extensions, but you will mainly use the already-famous active object for characters, backgrounds, enemies, or interface elements.

Create an active object and stay within the picture editor. The top bar on the left-hand side shows the tools you will need to import or save graphics from and to your hard drive.

When you click on the **Import** button, a file selector will open, allowing you to select the image file to import from your hard drive. According to the type of image or animation you import, you will be able to select either a simple image file or animation files.

For now, select any background graphic that you want to have in the platformer prototype and have created during the last chapters. A blue sky should do a great job.

The **Import** options will appear after you have selected a picture. These options are important to set the preferences of your picture, for you might want to import a single background picture, an image with transparencies, or even a full sprite sheet with an animated character.

The import options

You might have come across those sprite sheets already. They are used to minimize all the graphics of one animation to only one picture and optimize the file sizes of your graphics. You can check out http://opengameart.org to find some free sprite sheets like this awesome pixel explosion:

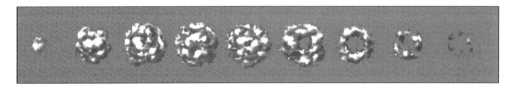

Back in the **Import** options, set the **Transparency** to any color you want to delete from your picture. In the case of our little explosion, the transparent color would be the pink background. Use the **Pick** button to choose another color directly from the image, or double-click the colored square to choose a color in a color selector. If you do not want to use a transparent color, simply choose a color that is not present in the image.

The import as animation options allows you to import a series of pictures as one animation. Just select the number of frames in the **Animation mode** options. It is important to name the single graphics chronologically in this manner: picture_01, picture_02, picture_03, and so on.

The sprite sheet option lets you import animations from sprite sheets. Set the block size to the size of one single sprite of your sheet.

The **Box mode** option allows you to capture several images contained in boxes in a single image file. In order for this option to work, you must respect some rules when saving the image file. First, every graphic you want to import must be surrounded by a rectangle of a color different from the background color of the image. The same color must be used to define all the rectangles surrounding the graphics contained in the image.

You will use all these options in your upcoming projects, but for now, we just want to import a simple background image without transparency or animations.

The active object has now switched from the green dummy diamond to your sky background. If you have placed the hotspot to the center of your picture, it should be at the exact same position of the former dummy graphic. Now place the picture to fill the background. It will overlay all your other objects, for it is the newest game object. Right-click on the picture, go to **Order**, and set it to **Back**.

No matter how big your background picture might be, scale it to 800 x 480. It should be larger than the frame now. This is exactly what we want for our next step: creating a parallax background.

Working with layers

Layers are very helpful for two main reasons. You can organize your frame and your screen using different layers for different objects. You can, for example, create an interface layer, a game layer, and a background layer to split up the graphical objects you will use within your game.

The layer properties are also important, as they allow you to add render effects (add, subtract, and so on) to your layer or set the layer movement speed (*x* and *y* coefficients) to create parallax backgrounds.

Open **Layers Toolbar** on the right-hand side. Create a new layer by clicking on the new layer icon. Now drag this new layer onto the existing one with all your current game objects. The existing layer is now the topmost layer.

Select your sky background in the frame and drag it onto the newly created background layer. No matter what, your sky graphic will now be behind any object of the top layer. Consider the following screenshot:

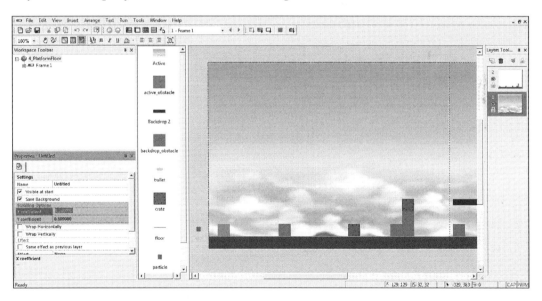

To add a parallax effect to the layer, just select the background layer, and set the x coefficient to something around 0.2. This will slow the background layer (and therefore the background picture) down to 20 percent of the top layer's speed. Feel free to test the parallax effect now.

The same effect will happen to the height when you set a value lower than 1 to the y coefficient. The layers toolbar will hide automatically after a while by default. It will stay open though if you pin it to the screen by clicking on the pin button to the top.

Now think of the possibilities of this effect. Create another layer between the top and the bottom layers, set the x coefficient to 0.4, and add graphics of a mountain or a hill. You will add a fantastic illusion of depth to your game.

Summary

In this chapter, you learned how to use the animation editor to create simple animations. You created a simple particle system and got to know how to work with the expression editor. You heard about the non-physical movements and how to use them in different game situations. You also know how to import graphics and animations and how to place them on different layers within your frame.

The next chapter will include the use of Fusions extensions and objects. You will also learn more about animations and how to implement them for a game object.

4
Using Extensions and Animations

The backbone of Fusion is its extension and objects system. In this chapter, you will learn how to import and use the advanced platform movement object. This chapter will also teach you how to use colliders and trigger animations.

In this chapter, we will cover the following points:

- Extensions and objects
- The platform movement object
- Colliders and character animations

Extensions and objects

One of the most essential systems of Fusion is the extension system. You have already used some built-in extensions or objects like the **Active** or the **Backdrop** object. Fusion already includes the most important and most common types. You can create them, as mentioned before, by double-clicking inside the frame in the frame editor. You can also right-click within your frame and choose **Insert Object**.

Besides those common extensions, you can easily add new extensions created by the Clickteam community. There are many spots where you can download extensions. I would recommend the official Clickteam forum:

```
http://community.clickteam.com/forums/205-Released-Extensions
```

To get an overview of all the current extensions, visit the following link:

```
http://dark-wire.com/store/extlist.php
```

In general, it is very easy to install an extension. After you have downloaded a new one, you can start the included auto installer, which would be the easiest way to install your new extension. Most extensions include two folders: `Data` and `Extensions`. Just copy those two folders to your Fusion directory. Overwrite the already existing folders. Don't worry—this will only add the new extensions and will not delete anything.

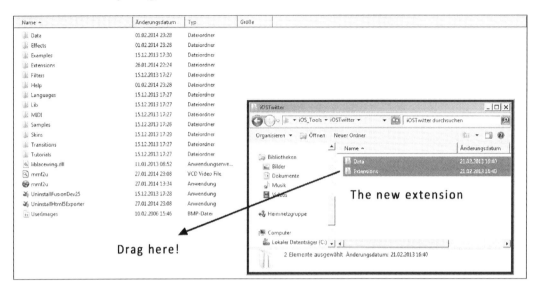

Drag here!

The new extension

Always remember

If you install a new extension, it will only work with the given exporter. If the author of the extension has created an iOS extension, then it will only work for iOS games. So always keep an eye on the export possibilities when you install an extension!

During your first few days of learning the tool, you will use more and more objects, and you will find out how and where to use the extensions or objects. We would need another book to explain all the possibilities in that case. So just play around a bit and don't be afraid to make mistakes. It is actually like what the great Bob Ross always said:

"There are no mistakes, only happy little accidents!"

The platform movement object

Talking about movements and extensions—there is another very useful, one-of-a-kind platform movement object. Create this very powerful extension just like an active object. It will control your character with much more accuracy and adjustable values.

The new movement

Create a **platform movement object** (**PMO**). You will not change this object directly, so you can place it somewhere in or outside your frame. Double-clicking on this extension will open up all the adjustable properties—but we will get to this later.

Set the movement of the player object back to **Static**. Now connect your player object to the platform movement extension in the event editor using the following line of code:

```
Start of frame - set object to player
```

The next thing you have to do is activate the collision between your player and the floor and obstacle objects again. You will need two conditions in that case, as follows:

```
Test for obstacle overlap +
Player is overlapping a backdrop
```

The following screenshot shows the platform movement object:

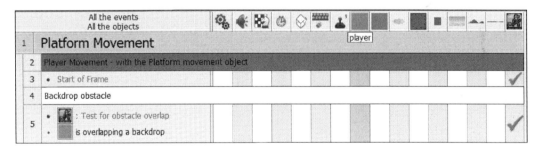

Your action will now take place within the platform movement object instead of the active object itself. Select the following action:

```
Selected object overlaps an obstacle
```

Your player object will now stop if it collides with the floor or the obstacles. Now you have to set the left and right movements. Remember, this can be done with conditions of the joystick icon, regardless of whether you use a joystick or the keyboard. Set the condition of this joystick object to:

```
Repeat while joystick is pressed right
```

Then set the action of your platform movement object to the following action:

```
User is holding right input key
```

Repeat the same procedure for the left movement. These events let your player walk left and right with the platform extension. Now you only have to build a new jump event. Select the action **Jump** in the platform movement object, for when the player presses `Button 1` as a condition. This can be done as follows:

```
Joystick Button 1 is pressed – Jump
```

If you test the movement, you will immediately feel the difference, especially when jumping over obstacles. The collision detection is far more accurate than with the built-in platform movement. Maybe you have also realized that double jump is also enabled!

Double-clicking on the platform movement object will open the properties of this extension. You can adjust the x and y velocities, the gravity, the jump strength, and so on. Your player movement is way more variable with this great extension. With a little time spent on tweaking, you can create nearly every platformer feeling you want:

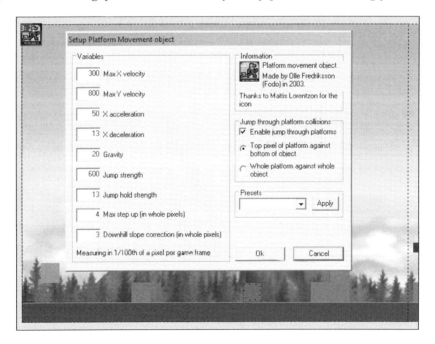

The best part of this object is that you can change the settings at any time. So just think of this example: when you want your player to enter a game area with low gravity, you just set the gravity from 30 to 10 and your player will enter a floating state! You will find out that this opens up a lot of new possibilities.

We can also use the implementation of this extension to set up a new direction for your characters. You might have experienced a bit of strange shooing behavior. This happened because you never set the exact direction of the player object. Now you can set the direction of your player object to the left and to the right when the player moves towards left and right! This specifies exactly two directions for the character, and your player will now face (and therefore shoot) only left and right and nowhere in between. The following screenshot shows this:

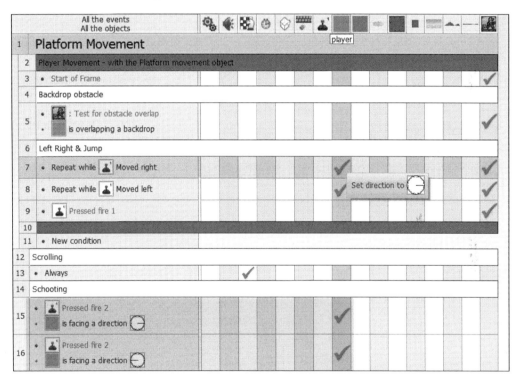

You can also use this extension for non-player characters or enemies. It's pretty useful for all kind of character objects in any side-scrolling or platformer game types.

Colliders and character animations

Currently, your player is a little green box. What you want, of course, is a walking character. For that purpose, you have to create a new object with all the animations you need for your actual character and put it on top of your former player object (the green box). This basic shape of the actual player is generally called a collider. It represents the physical body of the actual player but includes no animations as such.

Create a new active object and call it `player graphics`. Open the picture editor, and select the first frame of the **Walking** animation. This is where we want to place the walking sprites of our character. For prototyping purposes, download this free character from the following link:

`http://opengameart.org/sites/default/files/dino.png`

Import this picture to your animation editor. Choose the selection tool and select and crop every single walking step of our little dinosaur with the crop tool. You will get four frames (dinosaur sprites) that will be our walking animation. Select every single frame again and hit the crop button again. This will delete the remaining free space around the single sprites. Try to be as accurate as possible when working with the animation editor and imported graphics. It is important to also set the hotspot of every frame to the center to create a good-looking, loop able walking animation as follows:

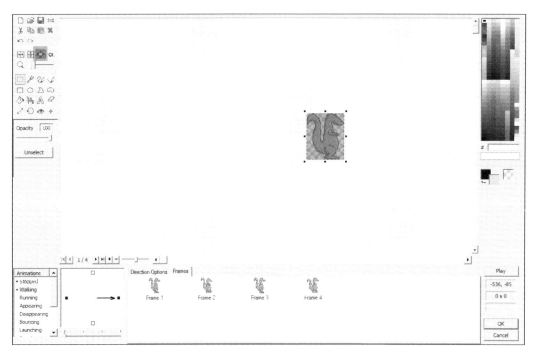

Now set the animation to **Loop** in the **Direction Options**. In this simple case, you can ignore the different speed values. The lower speed defines how fast the animation plays when the object is static. The higher speed defines the animation speed at maximum movement speed. Just set both the lower and higher speeds to a value of 12.

The dinosaur sprites are facing to the left. Select all the frames, and copy them to the **Left Direction** (16) of your walking animation. Now go back to the **Right Direction** (0), and flip all the frames horizontally as mentioned in the chapter before.

Copy the first dinosaur sprite to both left (16) and right (0) of the **Stopped** animation. This will be our **Standing** or **Idle** animation. Hit **Ok**, and close the picture editor.

The player collider and the actual player graphic should always fit together in size. Scale the dinosaur down to the size of your collider box if you want, or do the opposite: scale the collider up to the size of your dinosaur friend.

Walking animation events

Open the event editor and insert a new **Group** called `Player animation`. Create an **Always** condition and set the position of your new player graphics to the position of your collider. The dinosaur will now stick to the center of your green player box!

`Repeat while joystick is pressed left` should change the animation of the dinosaur to **Walking** and so should `Repeat while joystick is pressed right`. Also set the direction of the dinosaur graphics to the left and right when the player goes left or right. You can add this action in the same row of course.

If you test your game now, you will see that the walking animations will start when you press **Left** or **Right**. Now we only have to stop this animation when nothing is pressed. Duplicate the last event line (repeat while the joystick is pressed…) and right-click on the condition. You can set almost every condition to **Negate**. This will do exactly the opposite of the actual behavior—in our case: it will repeat when the joystick is not pressed!

Copy and paste the same condition in the same row, and set one to **Left** and the other to **Right**. Those two conditions should set the **Animation** setting of the dinosaur to **Stopped**.

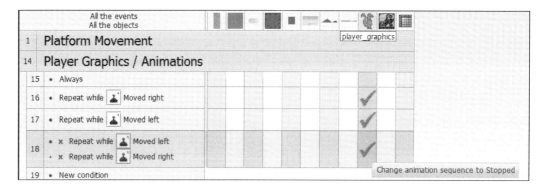

The left and right keys will now trigger the **Walking** animation. Pressing no key will trigger the **Stopped** animation (idle).

This is basically how you can switch between every animation you want. You can add a **Jump** or a **Duck** animation. Remember your dinosaur is able to shoot bullets. Why not add a shoot animation from its mouth?

Summary

Now you know about the use and possibility of extensions. You have worked with the very powerful platform extension and know how to use it. Now you know the advanced method of creating a platformer character movement.

You also learned how to construct an advanced character with a collider and a graphic object and how to trigger animations.

The next chapter will teach you how to use alterable values and counters to create a basic interface. You will also hear about simple enemy behaviors.

5
Creating Enemy Behavior and Health Bars in the Right Resolution

Game development is not all about turning cool ideas into games. You will also face a big non game-related technical part and a preproduction phase behind every game. Deciding on a resolution and the right interface for your game will be part of this chapter. You will also learn some basic enemy behavior.

In this chapter, we will cover the following points:

- Setting the resolution
- Introducing a new game type—top-down
- Enemy movements
- Alterable values and qualifiers
- Interface, counters, and health bars

Setting the resolution

Something we have not talked about yet is resolutions. Depending on which platform you're going to make your game or app for, you have to choose one or more possible resolutions. Let's say, you just want to create a little top-down shooter for a Windows computer. You don't need a fullscreen game and you are totally fine with the window mode. Great! Choose any resolution you enjoy—640 x 480 would be a great example as it will be small enough to be viewed on any computer. Of course, 640 x 480 is pretty low resolution these days. Things are getting more complicated if you think of a full screen computer game. Perform the following two steps to change the resolution:

1. Go to the application properties, scroll down a bit, and select **Change Resolution Mode** from the **Full screen** tab.

2. Select **Resize display to fill window size** from the **Options...** tab.

This will automatically scale your game window up to fullscreen no matter what resolution. Of course, this might squash or stretch your graphics depending on the size and aspect ratio of your screen. This might slow down your application a bit. Deactivate the resize option to keep the aspect ratio in between black borders as shown in the following screenshot:

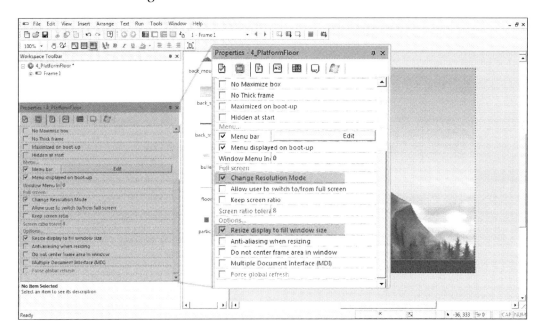

Now think of a mobile title. A ton of resolutions seem to be out there these days. Here, we mention a few examples:

Device	Resolution	Aspect Ratio
iPhone 4	960 x 640	16:10
iPhone 5	1136 x 640	16:9
iPad 4	2048 x 1536	4:3
Galaxy S1	800 x 480	5:3
Galaxy S4	1080 x 1920	16:9
Galaxy Tab 3	1920 x 1080	16:9

The resolution will reach ridiculous heights within the next few years. You can be sure that while I am writing this book, 10 new devices with 10 new resolutions will be released. Indie game developers cannot always produce games for all possible resolutions. Visit the following link for a list of resolutions of the most recent mobile devices:

```
http://www.binvisions.com/articles/tablet-smartphone-resolutions-
screen-size-list/
```

You can select the most common aspect ratios though (such as 16:9, 16:10, and 4:3), and optimize your game for it. The iPhone 4 with its 960 x 640 resolution has an aspect ratio of 16:10 for example. So, no matter what resolution you are working with, your game will not be stretched or squashed for that resolution. Of course, the variety of common resolution is growing too. You see, the resolution topic could fill half a book, but for now, let's head towards our next little game!

Introducing a new game type – top-down

We want to start a new little game prototype for this next chapter. Let's create a little top-down shooter. For that reason, create a new application. For now, let's choose one of my favorite resolutions for retro games: 480 x 320. Here are the steps to create a basic top-down character:

1. Click on **Application** in the workspace toolbar, choose Window in the properties, and select 480 x 320.

2. You'll be asked to apply these settings. Your application's resolution has been set.

3. Now set the size of your frame to 800 x 600 to create more space for your game objects.

4. Create an active object, center hotspot, and action point.

5. Set the movement of your object to **Eight Directions**, and change the properties to your desired values.

You have just created a basic top-down character that you can steer with the arrow keys (or later with the touch joystick if you want to create a mobile game).

Of course, you can also visit the Clickteam forum and search for a 360 degree movement example to get a more advanced movement system. In our case, the built-in eight-directions movement will do a great job though.

Create one more **Active** object. This will be your bullet. Change the graphics if you want to. Let's create a simple shooting event:

```
Repeat while "button 1" is pressed - Launch bullet in the
direction "player" with a speed of 100
```

Too many bullets are created while pressing button 1 now. You can trigger the bullets every 10 seconds with conditions from the timer. Just add the following condition to the existing button condition:

```
Every 10 seconds
```

This event will create one bullet every 10 seconds while button 1 is pressed. One more thing you could do is center the display at your player's position to activate scrolling just like in the platformer example:

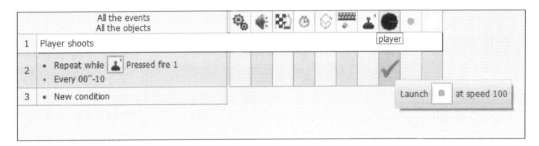

Enemy movements

As a next step, we want to create some basic enemy movements. Remember, this is just a prototype, so we don't really care about graphics. We just want to test different movements and events to get basic knowledge about Fusion.

The path movement

The simplest method to make your characters move might be on a path. Create an active object (an enemy), and set its movement to **Path**. Now hit the **Edit** button and place at least one node for a path. Also activate **Reverse at End**, and loop the movement in the **Path Movement Setup**. No matter what game type you are creating, the path movement can be used for a simple platformer enemy as well as for top-down spaceships.

The bouncing ball movement

The bouncing ball movement can be used for a million situations. The name that gives basic movement though would be another simple motion. Create an active object and set the movement to **Bouncing Ball**. Change the movement properties to whatever fits your game dynamic.

We want our object to bounce whenever it leaves the game area. You will only need one event to trigger this situation.

Start a new condition: navigate to **Set Position | Test position of "enemy"**. Hit all the arrows pointing outside the frame area in the pop ( ) up that appears. This will create the condition Enemy leaves the play area. Now select your enemy object and create the action—navigate to **Movement | Bounce**:

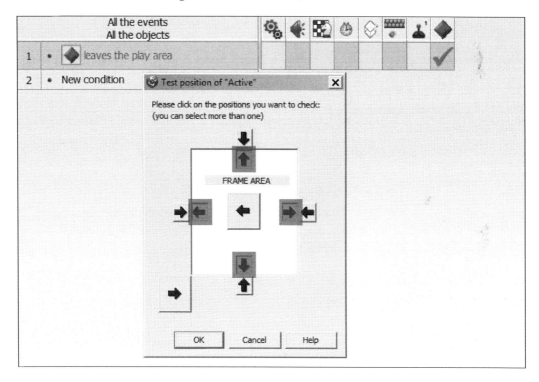

Just before your enemy object leaves the game area, it will bounce to a random direction within the frame. It will move forever within your game—until you blow it to pieces of course.

Direction detection – a basic AI

You can easily modify your bouncing ball enemy to follow your player object wherever it might go and create your first little **Artificial Intelligence** (**AI**). That actually sounds pretty cool, doesn't it?

Use the bouncing ball movement for a new active object again. Set **Speed** to a low value such as 8. Go to the event editor and create the condition **Always**. Select your enemy object to create the action—navigate to **Direction | Look in the direction of…— ( )** and select your player object. You should get this event:

```
Always - Look at (0,0) from "player"
```

The following screenshot shows the creation of the preceding event:

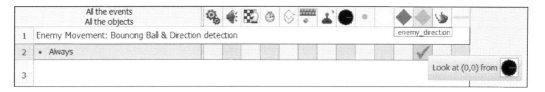

Your enemy moves with a constant speed of 8 towards the player now! This might be the most simple AI you can create with Fusion. The great thing is it totally works for simple enemies! You can always dig deeper and create a more powerful movement system, but sometimes less is more. Especially when things need to be done quickly, you will be very happy about the built-in movements in Fusion!

There are many, many, many different ways to work with the built-in movements in Fusion. There are just as many ways to create AI's for enemies and characters. You will get behind it step by step with every new game project!

Alterable values

At the moment, you have your frantic shooting player and a screen full of swirling enemy squares. Now we want to let them interact with each other.

In the next steps, you will learn how to use alterable values, which are internal counters you can change and make calculations with. In your special case, you will use those values for the health of your enemies, but they can actually be used for pretty much any situation where you need to set values. Some examples are as follows:

- Reloading the shield of a spaceship
- Money, gold, or credits of a character
- Number of bullets for a weapon
- Health, energy, or life bars

The easiest way to describe alterable values is with a simple example. We will give one of your enemies five health points, which is pretty nice of us.

Select the enemy with path movement and go to the **Values** tab in the objects properties. Hit the **New** button to create **Alterable Value A**. Double-click on **Alterable Value A** name it `PlayerHealth`, and set the value to 5:

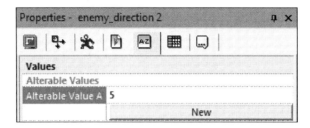

Naming alterable values is not necessary but is highly recommended. Each object has up to 26 values (from A to Z) by the way. The following screenshot shows the naming of alterable values:

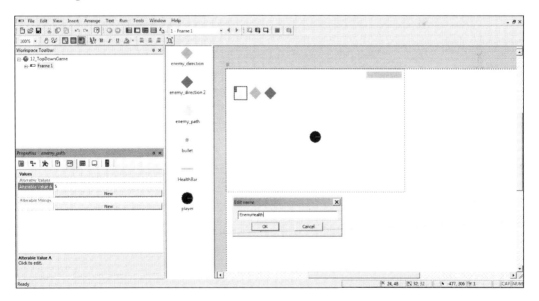

Now open the event editor to create the interaction of your bullet and your enemy. You will need a simple event that reduces the alterable value HealthBar by 1 whenever it gets hit by one of your bullets:

```
Collision between "enemy" and "bullet" - Sub 1 from "HealthBar"
```

Additionally, let this condition destroy your bullet.

The plan is to destroy the enemy object after it gets hit four times. To do so, test whether the alterable value HealthBar is lower or equal to 0 to destroy the enemy:

```
HealthBar <= 0 - Destroy "enemy"
```

This event will destroy your enemy when the alterable value hits a value lower or equal to 1. This is just one of countless possibilities for alterable values. As you can already see, alterable values will be your best friends from this very day!

Interface, counters, and health bars

We could talk a million years about good or bad interface design. The way your interface might look is just the beginning. Movement, speed, transparency, position, and size are just a few values you really have to think of with every new game. Some games completely go without an interface, which can create an even more immersive gaming experience. In other words, try to plan your interface precisely before you start to create an energy bar.

We will work with the **Counter** game object to create a basic energy bar. The **Counter** object stores the numbers in your application and is used for objects such as fuel displays, clocks, speedometers, and health bars. The **Counter** object can be displayed as an animation, a bar, or a simple number. You can also hide the counter if you want to use it for calculations only. The following is the screenshot of the **Counter** object:

Create a new counter object within your frame. The counter **Type** in the **Properties** settings is set to **Numbers** by default. Change the type to **Horizontal bar**. This will turn the counter to a small black rectangle. Change the color and size of this bar if you want. Now set the **Initial Value** to 10, the **Minimum Value** to 0, and the **Maximum Value** to 10. This means that the counter will start with a value of 10 when the frame (game) starts.

Assuming that the bar represents your player's health, values will be subtracted or added. The value of this counter cannot go lower than 0 or higher than 10, as we have set the minimum and the maximum values!

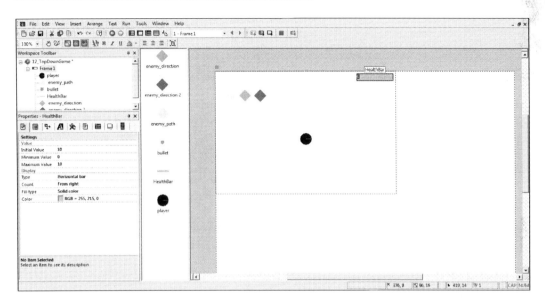

Now take a look at the **RunTime Options** tab. The option **Follow the frame** is important for every game. It is deactivated by default. That means that the counter will always stay in the same position no matter where your player character moves to. You can also put the counter (and the whole interface) in to a new layer of course.

Open the event editor and create an event that will subtract 1 from the **Counter** object `HealthBar` (very similar to your enemy):

```
Collision between "player" and "enemy" - Sub 1 from "HealthBar"
```

Also add a limiting condition to deactivate multiple collisions at one time. You'll find this condition under **Special | Limit conditions | Only one action when event loops**.

The only thing that is left is an event to destroy your object. Just test whether the health counter is lower or equal to 1 to destroy the player object:

```
HealthBar <= 1 - Destroy "player"
```

The following screenshot shows the event created:

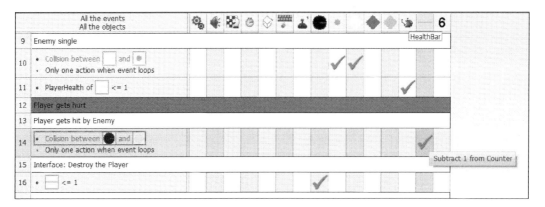

So, this is basically how you can use the counter object. As you can imagine, there are a lot of other situations where this object comes in very handy. You could, for example, create one more counter and leave it as a number. This could be your ammo counter!

Set both **Maximum** and **Initial Value** to 20 and the **Minimum Value** to 0. In the event editor, subtract 1 from the counter whenever your player character fires a bullet. Add the following condition to your existing shooting condition:

```
Counter > 0
```

Now your player will only shoot bullets when the counter is greater than 0. Of course, you have to add ammo packs to your game now. This is something you can find out on your own. Just use what you have learned so far.

Going further

Now think of the options you already have! You could add a destroy animation for your player. Let some simple particles bounce when your bullet hits the enemy or an obstacle. Go for some more advanced methods and change the animation of your player to a hurt state when he gets hit by an enemy. Maybe add some new events to your player. The player might be invincible for a while after he gets hurt, for example!

Also think of your previous platformer prototype. Create a counter and add 1 every time you destroy one of the red crates! Talking about the red ones: why not set a path movement to the red crates? This would turn them from static boxes to patrolling, evil, explosive crates!

Summary

Resolutions are something you will think about before you start your next prototype. You created a new game setup to test some more advanced properties. Your enemies are able to move and hurt now.

Within this prototype, you also created and placed your first interface and turned it into a basic energy bar for your player. Alterable values will also be very useful from now on.

The next chapter will cover the use of qualifiers and the highly anticipated physics. You will also learn how to implement sound and music in Fusion!

6
Physics, Qualifiers, and Implementing a Soundtrack

Learning the use of qualifiers is essential when working with many different objects of the same type such as enemies, weapons, or plants. To make your games scream, you will implement sounds and music in this chapter. We will also take a look at the basics of Fusion's physics!

In this chapter, we will cover:

- The use of qualifiers
- Integrating sound in Fusion
- Jump around - physics

The use of qualifiers

If you are using many objects of the same type, you are going to use a feature named qualifiers from time to time. A qualifier is actually just a small icon or name that can be applied to several objects. You can add the qualifier **Bad** to all your enemies even if you work with different objects. Qualifiers simplify a lot of programming. You can use one and the same event for all your enemies by attaching it to the qualifier instead of the actual enemy object.

You could have a robot, an alien, and a ghost in your level, and you want them all to run towards the player. All of them carry the qualifier **Bad**. The **Bad** qualifier should seek the player. This one line will work for every enemy with the **Bad** qualifier!

You should have at least three enemies in your top-down game example. Instead of repeating the same procedure for each and every enemy in your frame, we are going to use qualifiers to set some events for all the enemies!

Select all your enemies (mouse drag and select), open the **Events** tab in the object properties, and hit the **Edit** button to open the qualifiers pop up. Consider the following screenshot:

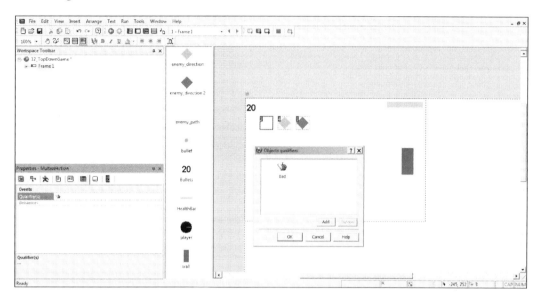

Now choose the **Bad** qualifier. Of course, you can select any icon you want. Qualifiers are just simple variables. The name or the icon has no direct effect.

All of your enemy objects should have their own qualifier now. We want them all to react in the same way as your single enemy object from *Chapter 5, Creating Enemy Behavior and Health Bars in the Right Resolution*. Every bullet will subtract one from its health bar. If this bar goes below one, the enemy will be destroyed. The only difference is that you will use the qualifier instead of the enemy object.

Try to add the `Enemy gets hit by player's bullets` event from the previous chapter to the **Bad** qualifier. Also destroy the qualifier if its alterable value **A** becomes lower than 1:

```
Collision between "Bad" and "bullet" - Sub 1 from "Alterable Value A"
HealthBar < 1 - Destroy "enemy"
```

The qualifier events will treat every enemy like an individual. When you test your level, you will see that all your enemies will be destroyed if you hit them four times with your bullets. Great job!

We also want the player to be hurt by an enemy. Open the event editor and create an event that will subtract one from your player's health:

```
Collision between "player" and "Bad" - Sub 1 from "Healthbar"
```

Remember to add the condition `Only one action when event loops` to limit the event. Without this extra condition, the player would be destroyed in the blink of an eye. Consider the following screenshot:

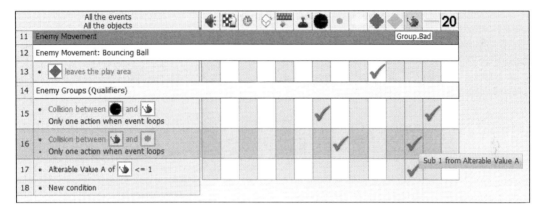

This was only one possible way to use qualifiers in Fusion. The more objects you will work with, the more you are going to use this great feature.

Integrating sound in Fusion

I guess by now you've already recognized that sound and music in games are not only an important topic for me but also to the small, quiet, game prototypes you have created so far. The atmosphere of your platformer would have changed had there been ambient cricket sounds. Just think how your **Topdown** blaster could sound like with bombastic "boooooms" while shooting, with a fast rock track!

It is actually pretty simple to integrate sounds and music in Fusion. The difficult task besides finding the right soundtrack is keeping track of the sound files, their positions, the increasing file size of your game, and so on. So here's the first rule: make a list of your sounds, create your own sound implementation system, and—guess what—plan your game sounds!

Game developers tend to either ignore or overuse sound and music. The trick is to use an adequate soundtrack at just the right time and position. Never forget that sometimes less is more.

Place your first sounds

We will talk about sounds or **sound effects** (**SFX**), music, and ambience or atmosphere (atmospheres and background sounds like a thunderstorm or rain). The soundtrack is the complete package of sounds, ambience, and music for a game.

Just to keep things clear, create a new application in the default resolution. Open the event editor and create the following condition:

```
Press fire 1
```

Now select the **Sound** section to create an action. You can choose between the **Samples** and **Music** options. You will mainly use samples in your games, so you can choose all kinds of sound files (`.mp3`, `.wav`, `.ogg`, and so on) as your game sounds.

The **Music** section will play classic **Musical Instrument Digital Interface** (**MIDI**) files. This might be of interest to you if you are into retro MIDI tracks.

If you have not already downloaded the example sounds, do it now from Packt Publishing's site. For now, select the option sample as your action and choose a sound file `sfx1`:

```
Samples-Play sample "sfx1" (Browse from a file)
```

The sound `sfx1` will start exactly once when you push button 1 (*Shift* by default). This is the simplest way to trigger a sound in Fusion. There are sound-specific extensions to integrate or modulate sounds, but to be honest, I would mainly use the integrated sound system of Fusion as it covers 90 percent of all the audio features you will need for a decent 2D game soundtrack.

The same single sound action can be triggered by collision of two objects or any other one-time event of course! For the next example, create two conditions in the same row:

```
Repeat while button 2 is pressed -
+ Every 10 Milliseconds (From the timer section)
```

These two lines will trigger something like a rifle sound every 10 milliseconds when button 2 is pushed. For that purpose, play the `sfx_hit` sample as your action. Holding button 2 will now create a nice "rat-tat-tat-tat" sound!

The next step will probably be background music or ambient sound. You will need a loop able sound file if you want to create a seamless, endless loop. For this example, use the included song `Intronition` as your background track.

Create an active object and paint a button. This will act as your switch to turn your music loop off and on.

At this point, you should learn another important mechanism of Fusion called **flag**. Flags can be seen as binary switches that can be either on or off. You can easily toggle between those two states in the event editor. We will toggle the flag 0 of our music button when the user hits it with the left mouse button:

```
Use clicks with left (mouse) button on MusicButton - Toggle internal
flag 0
```

Now you have to set the flag states. If flag 0 is on, it means that your sample is played in a loop. If flag 0 is off, it means the looping sample will be stopped:

```
Internal flag "0" is on - Play sample "Intronition" 0 times
Internal flag "0" is off - Stop sample "Intronition"
```

To make all these events more precise, add the already-famous and very helpful condition: `Only one action when event loops` to all three lines. Consider the following screenshot:

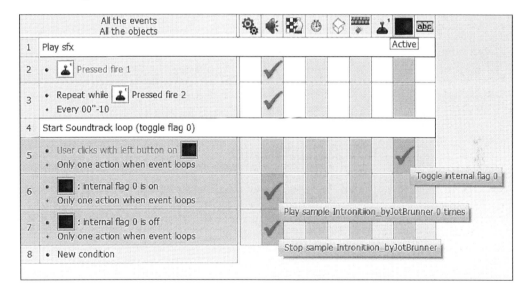

If you just want your song to play along with your game, trigger the endless loop with a `Start of Frame` condition!

Jump around – physics!

First things first: it is absolutely impossible to describe every detail of the physics objects included, which might be one of the most complex topics when working with Fusion. However, in this section you will get to understand the basics of the engine to go on your journey towards awesome little physics puzzles!

For a more detailed description of the single options, hit the *F1* key whenever you need more information. You can also learn a lot from the fantastic community:

```
http://community.clickteam.com/forum.php
```

Let's skip the definition of physics at this point. I am pretty sure you have played at least one physics title and know the basics of what those games look and feel like.

Fusion uses the famous open source Box2D physics engine and has implemented a highly-understandable extension and object system for all kind of physical situations. So let's go on and create some physically correct box collisions. Hooray!

Basic collisions

The physical movements can be used just like the non-physical movements by direct selection from the drop-down menu of an active object in the **Movement** tab. Even the behaviors of the classic movements, such as platform and eight-direction, are very similar and just as straightforward as the non-physical movements.

First, place the **Physics - Engine** object in your frame like you would create an active object.

This object will handle all your physics movements. You can compare it to a way more advanced platform movement object. Open the **Settings** tab of this object to play around with the general gravity or friction of your game scene. Now follow these steps:

1. Create an active object, paint a little box (or import graphics), and center the hotspot.

2. Set **Movement** for this box to **Physics - Static Movement**.

3. Create a backdrop object and a floor (don't forget to set it to **obstacle** in **Runtime Options**).

4. Open the event editor and create the following two events:

```
Box collides with background - Movement "Stop"
Box collides with Box - Movement "Stop"
```

5. Duplicate your box three or four times and start the frame (*F7*).

All the boxes will fall down in the given gravity. They will collide physically correct with your floor set to an obstacle. This little example displays the core of a physics engine: objects behave just like they would in the real world.

By the way, the use of qualifiers is advisable if you want to create different types of physics objects with the same basic behaviors.

The Physics movement

Create a new active object. Set the movement to **Platform** (we will only talk about physical movements in the next few steps). Placing the hotspot is essential to define the lower borders (the feet) of your player object.

You will quickly realize that the behaviors you have already learned, On collision with backdrop - Stop movement, will also work with the physics platform movement.

Take a look at your player's properties. In general, the properties of all the physics objects are pretty much the same. **Speed, Acceleration**, and **Deceleration** work similarly to the Clickteam platform movement object. The jump, crouch, and climb options will tweak the strength of those exact conditions. The density describes how heavy an object is. The mass of the object will be calculated from the surface of the object and its density.

The value **Elasticity** can be described as the bounce level of the object. The gravity scale controls how much of the global (world) gravity is applied to the object.

The engine will automatically detect the size of your active object and set it to an invisible physics collider for the object.

The Physics objects

You already know the **Physics – Engine** object. It needs to be placed in every frame when you want to use any kind of physics. So, creating this object is essential if you want your player object to run or stop, or want your boxes to fall down.

Some of the other physics extensions are instantly manipulating all your physics objects without any event after you have placed them in the game frame.

Let's start with the physics particles. Create one of these in your frame and start the level. Rainbow balls will start jumping all over your screen. This object emits particles from its center in all directions. With a little tweaking, you can set this emitter to behave just like you want it to. Lower the initial speed and set the angle to only two directions, and you will get a fine beam of colors. Change the particle graphics (just as you would change the style of an active object) to blue and white, and you'll get a waterfall!

The objects **Magnet**, **Fan**, and **Treadmill** will manipulate all your physics objects. If you place the **Fan** object below your waterfall particles, some particles will float in the direction the fan is oriented.

The **Treadmill** object will just work like a real conveyor and transport your object (particles) to the selected direction. The **Magnet** object tries to catch and manipulate the objects in its surroundings.

The rope and chain object

This object creates an awesome rope with chain elements and a heavy end pretty similar to a morning star. The chain starts directly at the center of the object itself. This not only looks great, but you can also attach objects (such as a player) to the rope:

```
Start of frame - Rope & Chain - Climbing - Attach "Player" to rope at
a given element
```

The given element would be your chain element of choice.

The ground object

This fantastic object allows you to define the shape of your physical ground. You can easily draw any shape of ground by creating the object somewhere at the bottom of your screen. Now duplicate the object (copy and paste) as many times as you need to in order to define the shape of your floor.

All the duplicated objects need to be instances of the first ground object! The final ground shape will be treated as a simple background object, so you can set the condition `collision with backdrop` just like in all the platformer examples before!

Consider the following screenshot:

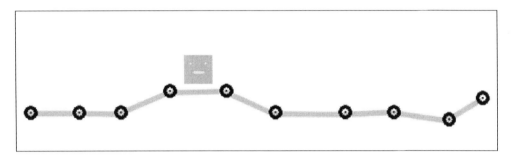

A simple trick to visualize the physics ground is to create a screenshot of your ground objects, import it to the picture editor of your choice, and connect the dots with simple lines.

The joint object

The joint object is a bit too complex and would go beyond the scope of this beginners' guide. Joints can constrain objects to each other or to the game world. Good examples of joint objects in games are ragdolls and trolleys. You can also add a motor to your joint. This will automatically rotate your object and could perfectly serve as a car wheel!

With all the knowledge you have gathered so far, I am sure you will find out about the use and the power of the joint object yourself.

Always remember, getting these objects to work as you want them to takes a lot of tweaking. But, in general, working with physics objects is very straightforward.

The Physics playground

The files that come with this book include a basic physics playground—just a basic example with a lot of physics movement happening. Maybe you remember the game *Incredible machines*. This game was not only challenging, it also exalted the imagination of thousands of people while fooling around with this awesome sandbox game.

The idea behind your own Fusion's physics playground or, actually, any Sandbox situation is to get creative and most importantly, to have fun! First, play around with all the possible physical values of all the awesome physics objects. Then try to think of a simple game mechanics you could build with all the new knowledge. Then you could think of a small prototype such as placing three **Ventilator** objects in the right position to move a particle stream from point A to point B. Always try to see the full picture when developing games and remember, sometimes the best ideas hide beyond the picture frame.

Summary

You have learned the basics of the Fusion's physics system and now know how to use the implemented objects. Physics is great fun but complex to understand. Take your time to fool around with the engine from time to time.

Qualifiers are very helpful when working with different objects of the same kind. They will simplify your events from now on.

Music and sound might be one of the most underrated topics in game development. Never underestimate the power of a great soundtrack and choose your sounds wisely!

In the next chapter, you'll learn to create mobile-specific applications and to create a simple save and load system.

7

Creating Loops and Saving Games

It's time to create a complete game! Learn to build a game from the start screen to the result screen, including one of your already created game prototypes. You will also learn how to load and save statistics in your game with the INI object. Global values and simple fast loops will also be covered in this chapter.

In this chapter, we will cover:

- Creating a basic game loop
- Global values
- Saving and loading with the INI object
- Fast loops

Creating a basic game loop

Up to this moment, you have only created a single frame each time you've started a new prototype. In other words, you only had one level of a basic game type. What you want to create, of course, is a game with all its features: a start menu, a couple of levels, a high score screen, and also the ending credits! You may even want to add your own game company's splash screen!

Creating a game with three frames

All the single game elements can't be placed in a single frame. You have to create a single frame for every screen, level, or menu that you want to have within your game. To demonstrate a complete game flow, open the last state of your platformer example.

Feel free to modify your game of course. Add sounds, add effects, and add whatever you like; always remind yourself: this is your game!

What we want to create are the following frames:

- Start screen
- Game (level)
- Game over or result screen

To create a new frame, click on the **Application** icon in **Workspace Toolbar**, and select **New Frame**. You should definitely rename the frame by right-clicking on the frame and selecting **Rename**. You could also rename your frame in the storyboard editor by double-clicking on the frame title. You can change the order of your frames by dragging them on top of or below your existing frames. Consider the following screenshot:

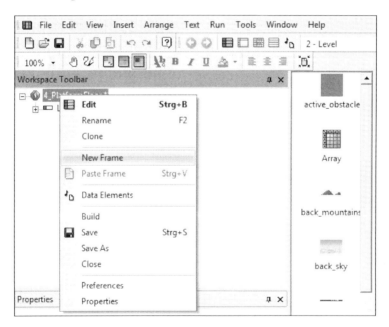

This new frame will be your start screen and should be placed on the first position of your application. Rename this first frame StartScreen. Frame 2 should be your actual game level—the shooting dinosaur. Name it Level1.

The start screen

Of course, the start screen or the start menu is essential. Let's keep it simple this time. Create a colorful background of the newly created frame. Maybe add a nice logo for your game. Of course, you need a button to start your level. You can choose pretty much any object as your button as long as you create the right event. For now though, create an active object and start with this condition:

```
User clicks with left button on "active object"
```

Then select the following action from the storyboard controls column:

```
Jump to frame number 2
```

Clicking on this button will now open frame number 2 when you are running the game. Frame 2, as mentioned before, should be your dinosaur level. In other words, you will start your dinosaur level after hitting the **Start** button in your start screen. To test these first steps, hit the *F8* key. *F8* will always start the full game, including every frame. As mentioned in *Chapter 2, The Editors of Fusion – Your First Game!*, *F7* will only start your current frame. The *F8* key will start the complete application!

The result screen

The result can be a goal screen, a game over screen, or anything in between. Create a new frame and name it `result`. Now it's time to tell the player of your game that he or she is awesome and has done a great job in achieving your game's goal!

Create a string object to create a goal message. This object type displays text you can edit and format in a variety of ways. You can display one sentence or several paragraphs in all fonts, sizes, and colors. Also, the movement, visibility, and position of the text can be changed easily. This object is mainly used for storing and displaying strings just as the counter object stores numbers.

Now double-click on the string, and write whatever you want to tell the player at the end of your game. The **Well Done!** message would be a great start. Consider the following screenshot:

Now you just have to create a button of any kind again to return to the start screen (frame 1). Congratulations! You have successfully created your first complete game loop! Press *F8* again to play your masterpiece.

We have kept things simple and clear for this example. For most of your upcoming games, you will need more than those three frames. You'll create options, menus, more levels, cut scenes, and so forth. You could easily create a "game over" screen, for example, which pops up when your dinosaur hits one of the red crates with just the approach.

Global values

Most objects can be turned into a global object in the object's properties. An object set to global will keep and transfer all its statistics and properties in every frame that it is included in. This is useful in all situations when you want to bring a value from one frame to the next one. Global objects can be scores, lives, gold, or all kinds of other statistics you want to keep over more than one frame. You can easily activate this option for almost every game object in its **RunTime Options**:

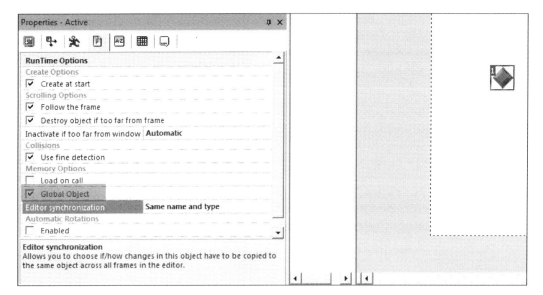

The **Editor synchronization** option will be set to **Same name and type** by default. This means that the engine will always look for the exact same object and name when you are working with the global object.

Consider the following example:

1. Place a counter on your dinosaur level and add one every time you destroy a box.

    Set this counter to global object and copy it (right-click and then select the **Copy** option).

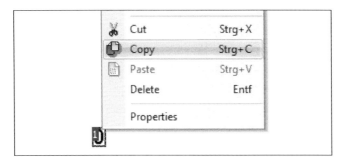

2. Paste it on your goal frame.

    You will see that it will show the exact same value as in your game frame!

A sneak peak – exporting your game

The next chapter will cover the basics of the export possibilities of Fusion. Just for the fun of it, we want to take a little leap forward and export your created game as a standalone .exe file. To do so, perform the following steps:

1. Navigate to **File | Build | Application**.

2. Choose a destination for your file and hit **Save**. Consider the following screenshot:

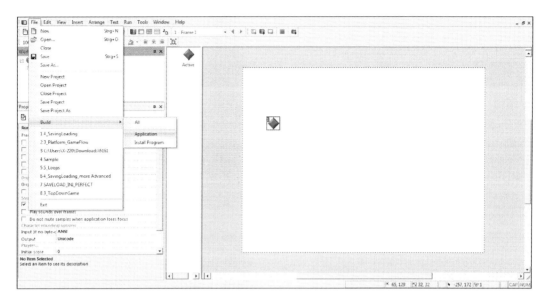

That's it! You have successfully exported your first game, and it can be played on any computer that runs Windows.

Saving and loading with the INI object

There is nothing better than a spontaneous game session without any pressure to reach a score or increasing the level of your character. But sometimes—well, let's face it—most of the time you will want to save your game statistics, your hero's progress, or just a new high score! This will be the moment when you need a saving and loading system.

There are some third-party extensions that can easily save your game statistics with one single event. But most of those extensions might only work with one single export module (Windows only for example). So if you want to play safe, use the INI object!

The INI object is a simple, text-based file that can store any value or string (number or text). It provides a simple way of saving information for future use. You can use INI files to save a player's status, location, or score. The values will be saved into a .ini file on the disk of the device.

Saving positions

To save your positions, perform the following steps:

1. First you need to set your INI file.
2. Double-click on the INI object.
3. Enter the name `save.ini` as your INI file. All the statistics you're going to save will be stored in this file.
4. Create a button and name it `Save`. This will be your general save button.

The simplest values to save are the positions of an object. Create an active object and set the movement to bouncing ball. Change the speed to something around `10`. Open the event editor and start with the following condition:

```
Button "Save" is pressed
```

Choose the INI object and create the following action:

```
Save position of "active object"
```

This event has just saved the *x* and *y* coefficients of your active object. To load the position, create this condition:

```
Start of frame
```

Choose the INI object again and create the following action:

```
Load position of "active object"
```

In other words, the position (and later on all the saved statistics) will be automatically loaded when the frame starts. Give it a try and hit *F7*.

Saving a single value

There is more than one way to save values and strings with the INI file. The next examples should show you how to save the value of a counter with a few simple event lines.

The easiest way is to save only one value to your INI. So if there is only one value to save (the value of a counter, for example), you can set the INI to the counter's value. The INI file will only save and load this one value.

To test this basic saving system, create a counter and add the following event:

```
Every 10 milliseconds - Add 1 to counter
```

Now create a simple save button and create the following condition:

```
User clicks with left mouse button on "save button"
```

Now add the following action to your INI file:

```
Set value to - counter - Current value
```

This event will actually save the value of your counter in the INI file. We want to load this value to your counter when the frame starts:

```
Start of frame - Set counter to: value of( "Ini" )
```

Consider the following screenshot:

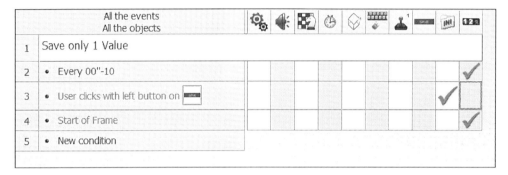

	All the events All the objects										
1	Save only 1 Value										
2	• Every 00"-10										✓
3	• User clicks with left button on [save]								✓		
4	• Start of Frame										✓
5	• New condition										

Saving multiple values in items and groups

If you want to save more than one value, you need to expand to the item classification. This means you name items (health, speed, dexterity, and so on) and set your values based on those names as follows:

- Health = 100
- Speed = 50
- Dexterity = 10

The cleanest way to save the statistics of your game, though, is working with groups and items. You could compare this to the folder system of Windows. Your group will be the main folder, which includes some subfolders (items), which in turn include the files (values).

The INI files will store values inside the named items, which are placed inside groups. This is useful whenever you want to save different type of statistics in different groups such as your player's statistics, your enemy's statistics, and your options as follows:

- Group = playerstats
    - Health = 100
    - Speed = 50
    - Dexterity = 10

- Group = enemystats
    - Life = 10
    - Speed = 50

Let's create a basic example. For this reason, create an active object (your player) and a new counter. Now add the following event to add 1 to your new counter whenever the player character gets hit by your mouse cursor:

```
User clicks with left button on "player" - Add 1 to "counter_health"
```

Now we want to save the new counter's value in the **playerstats** group to an item named **health**. You can use the **Save** button from the value example to create a new condition:

```
User clicks with left mouse button on "save button"
```

Add the following action to your INI file:

```
Set value (group - item) to "playerstats", "health",
value ("counter_health")
```

Your value has been saved to the item named **health** in the **playerstats** group! Now it's time to create the event to load these statistics:

```
Start of frame - set counter to...
```

Now select the following option from your INI file in the expression editor:

```
Get value (group - item)
```

You will realize that these lines pop up in the expression editor:

```
GroupItemValue( "Ini", >Group name<, >Item name< )
```

You just have to fill in the right variables inside the brackets:

```
GroupItemValue( "Ini", "playerstats", "health" )
```

Consider the following screenshot:

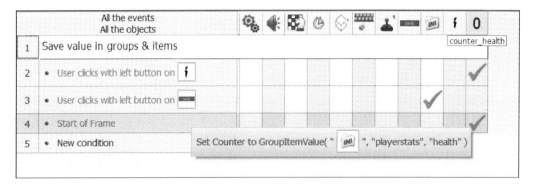

Start this example. Add a few hits to your player's health counter. Hit the **Save** button and reload the game. You will see that the value has been saved correctly.

If you want to add a new item (speed, for example) to your group **playerstats**, the INI action will look like this:

```
GroupItemValue( "Ini", "playerstats", "speed" )
```

This is basically how you can save and load tons of statistics in a very comfortable form. The naming conventions are important as usual. Name your groups and items wisely. You will be happy about that when you are working with many statistics. You will find a simple example in the download section of this book of course.

Fast loops

Loops (or fast loops) are used to repeat actions very fast a certain number of times. When a loop has started, it will repeat anything from testing variables to creating objects *x* times. This can be useful for a good deal of purposes like creating *x* background objects (stars, rain, trees, and so on) or adding a number *x* times to a certain value. To demonstrate this pretty simple procedure, perform the following steps:

1. Start a new application and create an active object within the frame.

2. Open the event editor and create the following condition:

   ```
   Start of frame
   ```

3. We will create a loop when the frame starts. The loop should run exactly five times.

4. Create the following action for your `Start of frame` condition:

   `Special conditions – Fast loops – Start loop "create" (create is the name of the loop) – 5 times`

   What we want the loop to achieve is to create five active objects at random positions all over the frame when the level starts. As mentioned before, this can be useful for creating random background properties such as trees and hills.

5. Create the following new condition from the special conditions:

   `On loop "create"`

6. Create this action in the `create new objects` column:

   `Create "active object" at 0, 0`

7. When the loop starts, five active objects will be created at the *x* and *y* positions 0, 0. To automatically place these newly produced objects all over your frame during the loop, add two more actions at your active object:

   `Set X position to "active object" to Random (640)`
   `Set Y position to "active object" to Random (480)`

These actions will position the five active objects created at random positions of your frame's height and width (640 x 480).

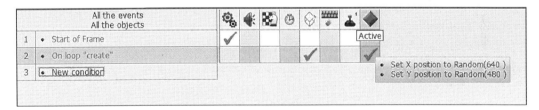

This simple example illustrates the power of fast loops. You will surely find plenty of situations where loops might be useful!

Summary

You learned how to create a basic game loop from the start menu to your game, including a game over screen and a back screen. Saved games are essential for most games; you know how to save and load statistics and values for your game now! Also, the essentials of fast loops and global objects are something you can work with from now on.

The next chapter will tell you more about the exporting possibilities of Fusion. From Windows to iOS to HTML5, Fusion is able to export your games and applications to a wide range of platforms.

8
Exporters of Fusion and Mobile Development

You have already exported some of your prototypes as a standalone executable file. Now it's time to get to know the other export possibilities of Fusion. You will also learn the basics of development for mobile devices.

In this chapter, we will cover the following points:

- Exporters of Fusion
- Development for mobile devices
- On the other side of the screen, it all looks so easy

Exporters of Fusion

Fusion lets you export your games and apps for a whole bunch of systems and devices. The basic version of the tool includes an exporter for the Windows executable files that you have already worked with. This file can be used on every current Windows desktop system.

Things get even more interesting when installing one of the additional exporters you can purchase for your version of Fusion. At the moment (we are talking about early 2014), Fusion can be upgraded with the following exporters:

- HTML 5
- FLASH (Swf)
- IOS
- ANDROID / OUYA
- XNA (Windows phone and Xbox)

You can be sure that Clickteam is already working on new export possibilities together with the community.

After you have installed a new exporter, you can easily select your **Build Type** via the **Settings** tab.

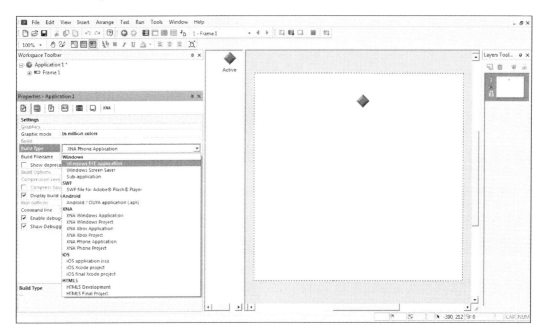

Each exporter adds its own special properties, while the basic properties (window options, runtime options, and so on) stay the same. The exporter's special options can always be found in the last tab of the properties window as shown in the following screenshot:

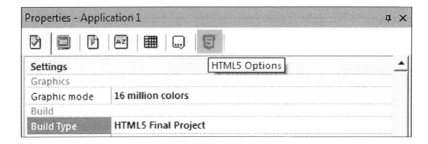

Every exporter also includes some special extensions and objects besides the basic objects of Fusion. Only the mobile exporter's (iOS, Android, Windows Phone) work with the **multitouch** and **accelerometer** (gyro sensor) objects, whereas the XNA Xbox exporter lets you use the Xbox Gamepad extension:

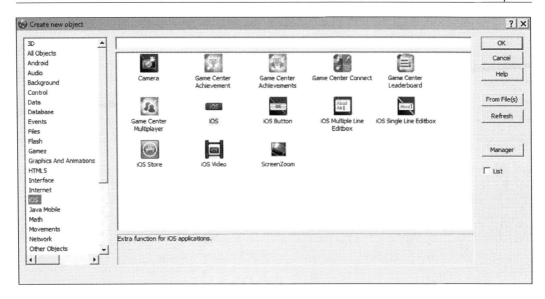

Flash (Swf)

The multimedia platform Flash is mainly used for creating animation, games, and (mostly) online applications. Flash games have surely crossed your way while surfing the web. Your export will deliver the .swf files right away!

HTML 5

Working with the HTML 5 exporter is another very popular way to create content for the online world. Your export will deliver the .html files right away!

If you want to create 2D games and apps for an online audience, both the Flash and the HTML 5 exporters are your upgrades of choice.

iOS

Although Clickteam Fusion 2.5 makes it simple to develop an iOS application, you will still need to understand the technique that apps use to find their way to the App store. You will also need a Macintosh computer running at least OS X Snow Leopard with XCode and with the iOS SDK installed. Last but not least, you need to enter the iOS developer program, currently available at 99 dollars a year, to actually publish your game. If you're a student, you can apply for Apple's University Program that allows students to develop on iOS and Mac OS for free! It might be a good idea to read more information about iOS development at the following link:
http://developer.apple.com/iphone/library/navigation/index.html.

Android/OUYA

Developing for Android devices (Smartphones or the OUYA gaming console) also requires a couple of additional tools, such as the **Java development kit** and the **Android SDK:**

- http://developer.android.com/sdk/index.html
- http://www.oracle.com/technetwork/java/javase/downloads/index.html

Publishing your games and apps on the Android market will be possible after registering a developer account, which costs 25 dollars.

XNA

The XNA exporter might be a bit more complex and diverse. You'll be able to develop for Windows phones as well as for Xbox.

Besides a Windows PC, a Windows Phone, or an Xbox 360, you will need an additional software, such as **Visual Studio** and the **Windows phone SDK** for your apps:

- http://www.microsoft.com/de-de/download/details.aspx?id=40787
- http://www.microsoft.com/de-de/download/details.aspx?id=35471

In the end, it's up to you which exporter (or maybe all of them) is your best choice. Decide whether you want to create games for iOS devices, online platforms, or consoles, and enjoy your days of developing!

Development for mobile devices

Thanks to the additional export modules of Fusion, it is very simple to create applications for most current mobile devices. Most events work in the exact same way you should be used to by now. One simple rule to remember when you are developing for mobile devices: a click is a touch.

This means that the mouse-click condition in Fusion is equivalent to a touch (also called a tap) on a mobile device's touchscreen. So whenever you use the following condition. It means that the engine will wait for a tap on the device's touchscreen. It´s as simple as that:

```
User clicks
```

Use this condition to create an event to jump to the next frame (game menu), for example:

```
User clicks - Jump to frame number 2
```

You can use the exact same method for tapping on an object (button):

```
User clicks with left button on "button" - Jump to frame number 2
```

File size and memory usage

When working on mobile titles, it's useful to approximately plan the file size of your final app. This is important for many reasons, but especially because you just cannot guarantee a perfect Internet connection to your customers.

It could take a while to download a game of 500 Mb without a decent Wi-Fi connection. So always try to optimize the graphic, sounds, and video files of your game.

Your games also might be slower on mobile devices (especially on older ones) than on your computer. Always mind the memory usage of your apps. Big pictures, sound or video files, frames full of unused objects, and so on are using a lot of memory. Try to avoid all of it.

Break your big pictures up into smaller parts to save space and so that a few of the pictures are shown in one frame at the same time. Use compression for your sounds and songs, such as mp3 or ogg. Here are the links to some free audio tools that might help you:

- http://audacity.de/
- http://www.freemake.com/de/free_audio_converter/
- http://lame.sourceforge.net/

Create your graphics in sizes of power-of-two to save memory. By power-of-two sizes, we mean sizes such as: 8, 16, 32, 64, 128, 256, 512, and 1024. This is because images have to fit inside their own texture. A picture of 832 x 799 still has to fit inside a texture of 1024 x 1024. So in this case, it might be a good idea to split the picture into smaller pieces to save memory.

Mobile control objects

Every exporter comes with some new extensions and objects. The ones you should care about in the first place can be found in the control section in the **Create New Object** window:

Accelerometer object   Joystick Control object   Location object   Multiple Touch

The accelerometer object

The **Accelerometer object** lets you use the built-in gyro sensor of your device to steer or control game objects by tilting the device. This can be useful from classic marble games to space shooters. You'll find a simple accelerometer example in the download section of this book, as an explanation of this pretty complex mechanic would take us too long here.

The joystick control object

You already know the basic joystick object of Fusion, which is controlled by your keyboard. You can activate an actual on-screen joystick for your mobile games via the **Options** tab of your frame's **Properties** window:

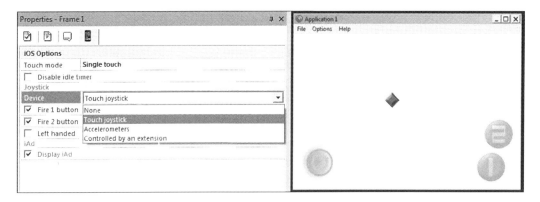

These on-screen touch devices will now work just like the arrow keys and the predefined buttons on your keyboard! Set an active object to eight-direction movement, export your game, and test the touch joystick. Additionally, you can create and use **Joystick Control object** to change the properties and variables of the on-screen joystick and its buttons.

The multiple touch object

Create this object to detect whether a touch has occurred. Yes, it's almost like detecting a mouse click, but this method is way more precise and faster than the basic `User clicks with mouse button` condition. Open the event editor and create the condition `Touch - A new touch has started` from **Multiple Touch** object:

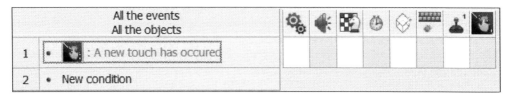

This object is also important if you want to work with more than only one touch (or tap). Just think of the pinch gesture to zoom in to or out of map applications! You need two fingers and, therefore, two touch points to create gestures like this. Similar to the accelerometer object, multi-touch with Fusion is a complex topic and would break the mold of this book.

The location object

The location object gets information from the built-in GPS sensor of a device. You can access the latitude, longitude, and altitude of mobile phones and tablets. Use this object if you want to create a simple GPS-based or map application.

On the other side of the screen, it all looks so easy

I hope you have enjoyed this short insight into game development with Clickteam Fusion. I also hope that the world will see a lot of your awesome little and big games in the future and that you really enjoy making games!

Oh… I almost forgot something very important: a statement, no, more an attitude to life by a great artist. Something you definitely need when your explosions just won't explode or your characters just don't know how to move the way you want them to:

> *"There are no mistakes, just happy little accidents"*

On that note, have a great life with game development, surprise us all with fantastic game ideas, and bring fun to the world!

Summary

This last chapter has given you a brief overview of the current export possibilities of Fusion. You have learned the very basics of mobile development and know where to find the most important mobile special extensions. And yes... we have quoted Mr. Bob Ross. What a day!

Index

simple particles
  adding, to crate explosion 36-38
sound effects (SFX) 68
soundtrack
  flag states, setting 69
  placing 68, 69
start screen
  creating 77
Stopped animation 24

T

top-down shooter
  Artificial Intelligence (AI) 58
  bouncing ball movement, using 57
  character, creating 55, 56
  creating 55
  enemy movements, creating 56
  path movement 56
Treadmill object 72

U

unique selling points. (USP) 6

V

value
  saving, INI object used 81-84
video game
  creating 5
  requirements 5, 6
Visual Studio 90

W

Walking animation
  about 50
  starting 51
  triggering 52
Well Done! message 77
Windows phone SDK 90
Workspace Toolbar 11
Workspace Toolbar, Fusion user interface
      11

X

Xbox Gamepad extension
  using 88
XNA 90

Thank you for buying
Getting Started with Clickteam Fusion

About Packt Publishing

Packt, pronounced 'packed', published its first book "*Mastering phpMyAdmin for Effective MySQL Management*" in April 2004 and subsequently continued to specialize in publishing highly focused books on specific technologies and solutions.

Our books and publications share the experiences of your fellow IT professionals in adapting and customizing today's systems, applications, and frameworks. Our solution based books give you the knowledge and power to customize the software and technologies you're using to get the job done. Packt books are more specific and less general than the IT books you have seen in the past. Our unique business model allows us to bring you more focused information, giving you more of what you need to know, and less of what you don't.

Packt is a modern, yet unique publishing company, which focuses on producing quality, cutting-edge books for communities of developers, administrators, and newbies alike. For more information, please visit our website: www.packtpub.com.

About Packt Open Source

In 2010, Packt launched two new brands, Packt Open Source and Packt Enterprise, in order to continue its focus on specialization. This book is part of the Packt Open Source brand, home to books published on software built around Open Source licenses, and offering information to anybody from advanced developers to budding web designers. The Open Source brand also runs Packt's Open Source Royalty Scheme, by which Packt gives a royalty to each Open Source project about whose software a book is sold.

Writing for Packt

We welcome all inquiries from people who are interested in authoring. Book proposals should be sent to author@packtpub.com. If your book idea is still at an early stage and you would like to discuss it first before writing a formal book proposal, contact us; one of our commissioning editors will get in touch with you.

We're not just looking for published authors; if you have strong technical skills but no writing experience, our experienced editors can help you develop a writing career, or simply get some additional reward for your expertise.

Learning Windows 8 Game Development

ISBN: 978-1-84969-744-6   Paperback: 244 pages

Learn how to develop exciting tablet and PC games for Windows 8 using practical, hands-on examples

1. Use cutting-edge technologies like DirectX to make awesome games.

2. Discover tools that will make game development easier.

3. Bring your game to the latest touch-enabled PCs and tablets.

iOS 7 Game Development

ISBN: 978-1-78355-157-6   Paperback: 120 pages

Develop powerful, engaging games with ready-to-use utilities from Sprite Kit

1. Pen your own endless runner game using Apple's new Sprite Kit framework.

2. Enhance your user experience with easy-to-use animations and particle effects using Xcode 5.

3. Utilize particle systems and create custom particle effects.

Please check **www.PacktPub.com** for information on our titles

Game Development with SlimDX

ISBN: 978-1-78216-738-9   Paperback: 150 pages

A fast-paced and practical guide on game development using SlimDX

1. Harness the power of DirectInput and XInput to detect and respond to user input from keyboard, mouse, and joysticks/gamepads while adding the all important interactivity to your games.

2. Make the most of Direct2D, DirectSound, XAudio2, and Direct3D to make your game worlds come to life on the screen.

3. A practical guide packed with example code and quick instructions on game development with SlimDX.

HTML5 Game Development with GameMaker

ISBN: 978-1-84969-410-0   Paperback: 364 pages

Experience a captivating journey that will take you from creating a full-on shoot 'em up to your first social web browser game

1. Build browser-based games and share them with the world.

2. Master the GameMaker Language with easy-to-follow examples.

3. Every game comes with original art and audio, including additional assets to build upon each lesson.

Please check **www.PacktPub.com** for information on our titles

Printed in Great Britain
by Amazon.co.uk, Ltd.,
Marston Gate.